TRAVELS

IN

GREECE AND TURKEY

BEING THE SECOND PART OF

EXCURSIONS

IN

THE MEDITERRANEAN.

BY

MAJOR SIR GRENVILLE TEMPLE, Bart.

IN TWO VOLUMES.

VOL. II.

LONDON

SAUNDERS AND OTLEY, CONDUIT STREET.

1836.

F.Rosenberg Sc.

CONTENTS.

VOL. II.

CHAPTER VI.

Purgasa — Lampsacus — Gallipoli—Constantinople —
View from the Mezarlek—Visit to the English Am-
bassador—Turkish Kaeeks—The Bosphorus—The
Sultan—His amusements . . *Page* 1

CHAPTER VII.

The Sultan—Pera—Perote Manghals or Brasiers—
Constantinople — Tomb of Abd-ul-Hameed—The
Vizeer's palace—Mosque of Aia Sofiya—Ancient
Hippodrome—Obelisks—The Nizam Jedeed . 32

CHAPTER VIII.

The Bazaars — Eating-houses — Wine-shops — The
Burnt Pillar and other Columns—Therapia and its

vicinity— General Guilleminot—M. Jaubert—Visit
to the Sultan   .   .   .   58

CHAPTER IX.

Remains of Old Byzantium—Ancient Cisterns—Aqueduct of Valens—Principal Mosques—The Suleymanieh—Tombs of the Suleymans—Benevolent Institutions—Universities—Lunatic Asylum   .   97

CHAPTER X.

The Army—The Nizam Jedeed—Cavalry—Uniform—
Manœuvres—Colonel Calosso—Barracks— Infantry
—Artillery—Military Hospitals—Russia and Turkey
—The Navy   128

CHAPTER XI.

Walls and Gates of Constantinople—Abattoirs—Church
of the Fish—Siege of Constantinople by Muhammed
II.—The Seven Towers—Visit to the Efendi's Harem
—The Eski Serai—Tekkehs of the Derwishes—Burial ground at Scutari   .   .   .   159

CHAPTER XII.

Departure of the Mekkah Caravan—Iskiudar and its
environs—Printing Office at Iskiudar—Leander's
Tower—Remains of Justinian's Villa—Daood Pasha
—The Sultan's Greyhounds—Tomb of Barbarossa
—Curious monogram .   .   . 190

CHAPTER XIII.

A Ball at the Ambassador's—The Seraglio Library—
The Baghdah Palace—St. Irene—The Mint—Sar-
cophagi — Bazaars — Bezesteens — Khans — Slave
Market   213

CHAPTER XIV.

Galata—Pera—Topkhaneh—Over-land passage of the
Fleet of Muhammed II.—Gibbon's Doubts—Statements of Saeed-ed-Deen and Evliya Efendi—Praises
of Constantinople—Return to Naples .   . 242

APPENDIX 259

TURKEY.

(CONTINUED.)

TURKEY.

(CONTINUED.)

CHAPTER VI.

Purgasa — Lampsacus — Gallipoli—Constantinople —
View from the Mezarlek—Visit to the English Am-
bassador—Turkish Kaeeks—The Bosphorus—The
Sultan—His amusements.

AFTER remaining here some days, and de-
spairing of ever seeing the wind turn to a
good quarter, we endeavoured to engage some
of the saccolevas, or small country sailing-
vessels, which were frequently passing up; for
these little craft, besides being famous for beat-

B 2

ing well to windward, can, by hugging the shore and using their oars, make way against both wind and current. We wished to engage one, either for Constantinople or only as far as Gallipoli, from whence we could have continued our route on horseback. We, however, found them all so full of soldiers and merchandise, as to render this mode of escape from our present position impracticable.

A Swedish ship lay alongside of us, having on board a giraffe, the largest I had ever seen, thirty horses, and four magnificent Egyptian asses, intended as a present to the sultan from Muhammed Aly, Pasha of Egypt. Lady Temple visited, in the cabin, the harem of the officer who had the charge of them. The ladies were natives of Egypt and of Habesh.

One day we walked to Purgasa, a village about four miles inland, prettily situated on the

side of a wooded hill, and surrounded by rich
and·productive gardens. The bazaar, covered
overhead by trellice work supporting luxuriant
vines, and filled with soldiers, caparisoned
horses, and peasants, for it was market-day, and
the *café*, crowded with fierce-looking Asiatic
soldiers and grave elderly Turks, smoking their
pipes, formed, on the whole, a very pretty picture. Purgasa, I imagine, occupies the site of
Percote, a town whose revenues were assigned
to Themistocles by Artaxerxes, to enable him
to furnish his wardrobe. In my ramble I found
only the cover of a sarcophagus, and a few fragments of marble.

Early on the 24th we were roused by the
loud but welcome sound of weighing anchor,
and were soon sailing rapidly up the Boghazi,
passing by Lamsaki, *(Lampsacus,)* an extremely pretty town. The houses were con-

structed in picturesque forms, with projecting
latticed balconies, and each house stood in a
garden full of rich foliaged trees, intermingled
with graceful poplars; near them dark masses
of cypresses, and white marble monuments
peeping through the openings, indicated mezarleks, or burying-grounds; whilst in different
directions, were seen rising in the air, lofty and
slender minarets of dazzling whiteness, surmounted by the gilt crescents of Islamism,
forming altogether groups of great beauty.

In ancient times *Lampsacus* was famous for
the dissolute habits of its inhabitants:

Quà domus tua Lampsaci est, quàque silva, Priape,
Nam te præcipuè in suis urbibus colit ora
Hellespontia ;

Catullus.

and it may, for aught I know to the contrary,
still maintain its former character.

Alexander the Great (to tell a well-known tale) having marched against it to punish it for some offence, Anaximenes, a native of the town, and who had formerly been the king's tutor, was sent by his countrymen to deprecate his anger. Alexander immediately suspecting the object of this mission, swore he would not grant the favour about to be asked. On this, Anaximenes entreated his pupil to destroy the town, and enslave the inhabitants, and thus saved *Lampsacus.*

Beyond, on the left, is Gallipoli, called by the natives Keleeboly, كليبولى, a large town, above which are the promontories of the Old and New Fanars; here the channel is very narrow. The difference between the two coasts now became very marked; whilst the Asiatic side was bold, varied, and wooded, the European was without trees, apparently barren and

low, so low indeed, that we saw over the Thracian
Chersonesus, and beheld the hills on the opposite side of the Gulf of Saros.

On the isthmus we observed a great number
of tumuli, either tombs or sanjak-depehs.

We had now left behind us the channel of the
Dardanelles, on different parts of whose length
are many strong batteries, mounting all together
seven hundred and fifty-one pieces of cannon,
namely, four hundred and twenty-eight on the
Asiatic, and three hundred and twenty-three on
the European shores—without including those
about to be placed on a lately erected battery,
which, I believe, was to carry thirty-two.

It is not my intention to discuss at length the
often agitated question respecting the practicabi-
lity of forcing this passage with a fleet. We have
certainly succeeded once in accomplishing this
feat, but many lucky and combining circum-

stances are required to render such an undertaking advisable ; so that I think we may safely
say that without them it is not practicable with
a fleet alone, especially if the forts and batteries are manned with a sufficient number of
well-disciplined artillerymen, and the men stand
by their guns. This, however, was far, in
either respect, from having been the case with
the raw levies, who were hurriedly sent down
to contend against the English. With a co-
operating land force the enterprise might prove
of easy accomplishment, as, from their situa-
tion, all the works could easily be taken by land.
A force might also be disembarked on the shores
of the Gulf of Saros above Gallipoli, where
the Chersonesus is only from four to five miles
in breadth, and across which runs a chain of
heights which would form an excellent position,
and prevent the arrival of any reinforcements

and supplies from the capital. On the Asiatic side the ground, which is hilly and broken, does not afford the same facilities.

At night we were alongside of the island of Marmara, *(Præconnesus,)* and in the morning close to the island of Papa, or Kalolimno, *(Besbicus ins.)* when we tacked and got back under Erkli, *(Heraclea;)* we then stood on, close in shore, passing by Silivri and Biuyuk Chekmejjeh, a long bridge, or rather four different but connected ones, having twenty-six arches. It was built by Suleyman the Magnificent, over the ancient *Athyras.* Some distance above it is a lake, and near it is a palace, to which the sultan resorts during the shooting season. Some way beyond is another bridge over the *Bathynias,* called Kuchuk Chekmejjeh.

We anchored off the point of St. Stefano, on which stands very conspicuously another of the imperial palaces.   The village itself is much resorted to in summer and during the plague, by the Christians.

Next morning we again proceeded, though very slowly, but every advance presented some new object of beauty or of interest, as the Great Imperial City, once the mistress of the world, gradually appeared.

The European with the Asian shore,
Sprinkled with palaces ; the ocean stream,
Here and there studded with a seventy-four ;
Sophia's Cupola with golden gleam ;
The cypress groves ; Olympus high and hoar ;
The twelve isles, and the more than I could dream,
Far less describe.

It was, certainly, one of the most enchanting and magnificent views it is possible for the imagination to conceive, and left far, far behind, all the rapturous accounts I had ever heard of it.

Passing close on our left the famous and
dreaded old fortress of Yedi Koullehler, (the
Seven Towers,) which forms one of the three
angles of Constantinople, and passing along the
old walls which still border the edge of the sea,
the brig anchored opposite the new Armenian
quarter; and we, getting into a boat, pursued our
way, doubling the Seraglio point, and entering
the harbour of the Golden Horn. Having
landed at the custom-house of Galata, called by
the Turks Othmanlu Kancheleria, we soon found
we were no longer in a Christian country; no
obstacles were thrown in our way, no search
took place, and no questions were asked, so that
having procured a guide, we walked quietly and
unmolested through the narrow and irregular
streets of Galata, ascended the "infidel hill"
of Pera, and soon after were comfortably
seated at supper in the *Locanda d'Europa*.

During the dessert, a Turkish officer attended by his orderly came to pay us a visit; they both sat down and seemed on very familiar terms with each other. Wine was offered to them which they refused, but drank with considerable apparent satisfaction a tumbler of cognac.

We were kept awake nearly the whole night by myriads of fleas, together with the noise of the watchmen striking the pavement with their iron-shod poles, and the incessant recitation of Arabic prayers or poetry, immediately under our windows by some sleepless lover or devotee. I endeavoured to free myself from this latter gentleman by pouring the contents of the water-jug on his head, but unfortunately for me he was either too entirely wrapt up in his occupation to be aware of what had happened to him, or, knowing it, was too great a philosopher to

mind it. At all events, he still went on re-
citing.

On the following morning, (27th October,)
we strolled about in different directions for the
purpose of obtaining a general idea of the surrounding localities. From the Mezarlek, called
by the Franks, *le petit champ des morts*, which
occupies the face of the hill rising behind the
Ters-khaneh, or arsenal, and crowned by the
palace of England, the view embraces the harbour, with the city of Stambool beyond. From
the *grand champ des morts*, the prospect is in-
describably beautiful and extensive, commanding a long range of the Bosphorus, covered, as
it always is, with numerous vessels of all nations and of all forms, besides actual swarms
of small, light kaeeks rapidly skimming, like
swallows, the surface of the water in all directions,—together with Kandilli, Beklerbek, Scu-

tari, Læander's Tower, the sea of Marmara, the
Prince's Islands, and other places. Below is
seen the palace of Beshiktash, the village and
palace of Dolmabaghcheh, and the adjoining
cavalry barracks; immediately to the right is
the great Turkish burial-ground, beautiful and
imposing from its sombre masses of venerable
cypresses, and, on the left, the Armenian cime-
tière with its smaller and lighter species of
trees. In the distance, on the right, rose
Mount Olympus, and on the left, the Giant's
Mountain, and the other hills which overlook
the Black Sea.

Mr. Seymour, secretary to the embassy, Mr.
Cartwright, consul-general, and Mr. Buchanan,
attaché to the embassy, were kind enough to
call on us; and, the following day, Mr. Villiers,
another *attaché*, also called, bringing a kind
invitation from Sir Robert Gordon, the ambas-

sador of England, to pass some days with him
at his summer palace of Therapia, to convey
us to which his kaeek was to be sent the next
morning; at the appointed time a Ghawas,
غواص, made his appearance, and told us
all was ready.* Following him, we descended
to Top-khaneh, where we embarked in the
kaeek.

Nothing can exceed, or even equal, the
elegance of these kaeeks, or the extraordinary rapidity with which they are propelled;
they draw so little water that they actually
seem to skim the surface, and only, *par
pure complaisance,* to touch the water in

---

* These Ghawases form the Serasker's body-guard;
and a certain number of them are attached to the
household of the several foreign ambassadors and ministers, and replace, in these functions, the old Janizaries.

their course. After having for a short time
been accustomed to view these graceful objects, even the neatest and lightest man-of-war's
boat seems dreadfully ugly and heavy, as it
awkwardly and laboriously forces its noisy
way. The kaeeks are excessively long, with
a sharp, elongated, and overhanging prow,
finishing in an iron point, and in shape resembling the horizontal section of a dolphin, the
tail-end forming the prow; the interior is lined
with walnut wood richly carved in relief, and
in parts gilt. At the bottom are cushions or
carpets, on which to sit with the legs crossed
à la Turque, the back being supported by
pillows of red leather: but the after part being
however raised, Franks are enabled to sit after
the manner of their country.

The kaeek we were in was pulled by three
men, each having a pair of oars or skulls: that

part of the oars which is inside the boat swells
to a large circumference, producing a weight
near the hands which greatly facilitates the
labour of pulling. The men were very handsomely dressed in crimson cloth open waistcoats richly embroidered with gold, a white
shirt with loose sleeves, and trousers of
snowy whiteness and most ample dimensions,
which, reaching only to the knee, left the leg
bare: the head, which is closely shaved, is surmounted by a very small, red scull-cap with
a blue silk tassel.

We flew rapidly along, in spite of the ad-
verse current; but, at Arnaood-keui and another place, it was so violent that we were obliged to be towed by men who station themselves at these places for that purpose. Passing by Dolma-baghcheh, (باغچه,) Beshik-tash,
(بشك طاش, "the stone cradle,") Orta-keui,

Arnaood-keui, Roomely Hissar, the Castle
of Europe, Balta-liman, Stenia, Yeni-keui,
several batteries, a prettily situated camp,
and the Sultan's favourite residence at Therapia, over which, being Friday, waved the
proud, blood-red, imperial banner, bearing the
Tooghra, طغرا, (the complicated cypher of
Sultan Mahmood,) we landed at the stairs of
the English Palace.

All the ideas I had formed of the beauties
of the Bosphorus* were much surpassed by the
reality. The European shore, surprisingly
lovely as it is, must still yield the palm of
beauty to that of Asia; but, on both sides, the
succession of pretty and picturesque villages,
lofty towns, and frowning batteries, imperial

* By the Turks the Bosphorus is called indifferently
Khaleeji, Kostanteeneah, Kara-deniz boghazi, and
Istambool boghazi.

palaces, and kioshks, private villas, the swelling domes and taper minarets of mosques,
the verdant foliage of numberless varieties of
trees and shrubs, the bold and graceful out-
lines of the hills, intersected in all directions
by smiling valleys, the beauty of the channel
itself, appearing more like a succession of
placid lakes, and the clearness of the sky, unite
in forming the most complete fairy scene of en-
chantment that can be imagined. This scene
has often been beautifully described by the
poets of the east, and, among others, by the
Turkish bard Malhemi, who thus prettily sings
its praises in Persian verse :—

شعب و غوطه و ابله و سغد

در جهان شهرتي جنان دارد

هر دو بو تاز شهر اسيانبول

در جنان شهرتي جنان دارد

" As Shab, and Ghootah, and Ablah, and
Soghd, are considered on earth as heavenly
cities, so are the two shores of Istambool renowned in heaven as celestial abodes."

Another author thus describes it :—" The
imperial capital of Constantine, which, at
the confluence of two oceans and two worlds,
resembles a diamond set between two sapphires and two emeralds, and forms the most
precious centre-stone of the ring of universal
empire."

The ambassador's house is a delightful summer residence, and is separated from the clear
and deep waters of the Bosphorus only by a
narrow quay. It commands a beautiful prospect of the Asiatic coast, and the Bay of Biuyuk-dereh, (" the great valley.") The back
is open, and looks on the garden, which rises
in a succession of terraces, (on one of which are

the Turkish baths,) to the summit of the lower heights.

Next day, we crossed over to Unkhiar-is-kelehsi on the Asiatic shore, and landing, found ourselves in a delightful valley covered with the finest rich turf imaginable, fully equal to that produced in our own humid country, and in parts shaded by large trees which would be an ornament to any English park. Here stands one of the Sultan's country houses, originally built by Selim III., as a kiaghd-khaneh (كاغد ـ خانه) or paper manufactory.

To our unexpected delight, one of the first persons we saw during our walk, was the Pad-shah himself (the Sultan) seated on the turf, under the shade of a large sycamore, and employed in shooting arrows up the wind. He was dressed in a plain, red beneesh, and was only attended by his favourite and chief secre-

tary, Mustafa Efendi, and a few eich-oglans,
or pages, to pick up his arrows.

The bow he used was made of horn, very
short, and much curved. He is said to be in-
disputably the best and strongest shot in his
dominions; and the numerous little marble
columns, which are seen on all the downs which
surround the capital, attest his most famous
performances, and bear convincing proof of
his prowess in archery.

This accomplishment is much in fashion here,
especially among the household of the sovereign; and indeed, most persons are in possession of bows and arrows.

Returning to the boat, we rowed along-shore,
passing under the Giant's Mountain or Yooshi-
dagh, and crossed over to Biuyuk-dereh, a
pretty and well-known village, inhabited by
many of the diplomatic corps. Off the Rus-

sian palace, lay the Princess Lovicz frigate
and a lugger, which were to convey to Italy
M. de Ribeaupierre, the Russian ambassador,
and his *suite*.   One of the frigate's boats, with
a lieutenant and six men, had just been upset,
and all had perished.

We remarked vast flights of those restless
and indefatigable birds, called by the Turks,
Marty-koosh, and by the French, *âmes damnées*.
They are a species of the *Alcyon voyageur*, and
are never observed to rest, but keep constantly
flying up and down the stream at about six
inches from the surface of the water.

> He wanders, joyless and alone,
> And weary as that bird of Thrace,
> Whose pinion knows no resting-place.
>
> *Moore.*

On the 31st of October we started with the

ambassador, on horseback, to visit the village
and forest of Belgrade, or, properly speaking,
Belighrad, بلغراد. Proceeding by the upper
road, which runs along the summit of some
ranges of heathy heights, we shortly came to
the commencement of the wooded region, and
then passed by the lofty aqueduct of Ibrahim
Pasha, which spanning the commencement of
the lovely valley of Biuyuk-dereh, forms so
pretty a feature in the landscape when viewed
from the anchoring-ground in the Bosphorus :
beyond this, we rode through the dirty Greek
village of Bagheheh, and soon after reached
Belighrad, also inhabited by rayahs. It consists of a small collection of scattered houses
prettily situated on a green turfy clearing, close
to one of the numerous bendts or reservoirs,
which supply, by aqueducts, water to the capi-

tal, and is quite embosomed in the midst of a forest of fine old trees. Some of the Frank families
of Pera have houses here in which they spend
the summer months; at one of them, at present
in a very dilapidated state, Lady M. W. Montague once resided.*

Sir Robert Gordon had prepared a *fête
champêtre* on the green in front of the village.
A large tent had been pitched, under which we
dined, whilst an Armenian band played several
Turkish airs, and some Greek men and women
from Biuyuk-dereh danced the Romaika, after
which a French band of musicians played several European pieces. Numberless but fruit-

* Her ladyship's powers of vision must have been
much more acute than mine; for she states that from
her window she discerned the waters of the Euxine,
notwithstanding that several high ranges of heights
must then, as they do now, have intervened.

less attempts were made to induce the village girls to dance, but all declined, some on the plea of being betrothed, others of being just married, but all evidently too bashful to exhibit their graces. However, they, as well as the dancers, were made very gay and happy by being allowed to draw with the ladies of our party, in a lottery of which all the numbers were prizes, and for which Sir Robert had provided a large quantity of turbans, kalem-khiars, yaghleks, kooshaks, bashleks, and trinkets, which were arranged in festoons from tree to tree. We concluded a very agreeable day by dancing within doors.

The following morning, mounting our horses, we dived into the depths of the forest, which is excessively wild and beautiful; and the numerous and luxuriant creepers which hang from every tree, and connect them together, greatly

add to the effect. Our course wound at times,
down deep dark and romantic dells and ravines, whilst at others, it led us to the summit
of comparatively barren heights, from which
we obtained extensive views of the surrounding
country. Having rode six miles, we found
twenty beaters assembled, when we dismounted
and took up our positions for the approaching
chasse.

The sportsmen were formed in extended line,
along the length of an elevated ridge, whilst
the beaters, descending from the opposite side
into the intervening valley, drove the game up
to the guns; and in this manner we went from
position to position. Several wild boars were
killed; our sport would however have been
much better, had not the lazy Greek beaters,
after the first hour, quietly and gradually returned home, leaving us at last with only eight

men, and these had become very lethargic in
the execution of their duty.

Arrived at Purgas, we again mounted our
horses, and galloped on to Justinian's aqueduct, where we met the ladies of the party
also on horseback, and with them returned to
Purgas, where we found a *déjeuner*.

In this part of the country are a great number of aqueducts, and bendts or reservoirs
of water, some of considerable antiquity, and
others dating their existence from Suleyman I.,
(who reigned from 1520 to 1566,) and subse-
quent sultans. The bendts are formed by very
thick and solid walls, tapering from the base
upwards, being built across a valley through
which may chance to flow a small stream of
water; some are extremely handsome, being
decorated with ornaments and inscriptions, and
have a summit of polished white marble

Many of the lakes which are thus formed, are of great extent, and are bordered by a thick growth of forest-trees; their edges are covered with a velvety and rich green carpet of turf, on which the deer are occasionally seen cropping the grass, or allaying their thirst in the stream. These waters abound with a great variety of wild-fowl during the proper season.

The greatest attention is paid to these aqueducts and reservoirs, for on them almost entirely depends the supply required by the capital; in fact, if these were ever destroyed, or in the power of the enemy, Istambool would fall an easy prey; for the water which could be procured from other places would not nearly suffice for the consumption of its inhabitants. Aware of this, the Turks, during the last war, threw up a few field works in their vicinity.

After remaining three days at Belighrad, we returned to Therapia, and stopped there also three days, previous to going to Constantinople. I shall, however, delay for the present giving any account of the numerous beauties of the surrounding country, as I was subsequently enabled to extend my rambles to several places which I did not see upon the occasion of my first visit.

CHAPTER VII.

The Sultan—Pera—Perote Manghals or Brasiers—
Constantinople — Tomb of Abd-ul-Hameed —The
Vizeer's palace—Mosque of Aia Sofiya—Ancient
Hippodrome—Obelisks—The Nizam Jedeed.

ON the 5th we returned to Stambool, and, as
it was Friday, we stopped on our way at Yeni-
keui to see the Sultan, who intended going to
the mosque of that village.* The whole shore

* I have never been able to discover from what
oriental word the Franks have derived this said name
mosque; for both in Arabic and Turkish these
buildings are called ﺟﻣﻊ Jamaa, signifying " a
place of assembly." The nearest affinity I can
find, is in the word ﻣﺳﺟﺩ Musjed, which signifies

from Therapia to Yeni-keui was lined with troops under arms, and in all directions was seen the simple but beautiful flag of the Othmanlus gaily fluttering in the breeze. We took our station opposite the quay where Sultan Mahmoud was to land. After waiting some time, the distant but gradually-nearing shouts of the troops announced the approach of his majesty ; and the imperial barge, followed by two others, was soon after seen rapidly advancing in our direction. The swiftness of its progress was absolutely astonishing ; for, built on a larger scale, but of the same proportions as the common kaeeks, it was propelled by four-

" a chapel ;" and, if we pronounce the ‎ح‎ or *j*, like a *g*, as the Egyptians do, we may perhaps trace some resemblance in sound. This letter is, however, by the Turks pronounced like the English *j*, and by the western Arabs like the French *j*.

c 5

teen athletic and supple-limbed rowers: (this
number, on state occasions and in a larger boat,
is increased to twenty-six :) the men were
dressed in loose, white-striped silk shirts, white
cotton shelwars, or trousers reaching to the
knee, and the little red scull-cap. The boat was
simply painted black with two gilt expanded
eagles, one at the stern, and the other on its
sharp and elongated prow. At the helm sat a
venerable Turkish pilot with a large, flowing,
grey beard, and a magnificent and well-ar-
ranged Asiatic turban.* This personage is the
only *employé* in the Sultan's service who still
is allowed, notwithstanding all the late innovations in costume, to retain this truly-distin-
guishing and becoming head dress.

As his boat passed within three yards of ours,

* Our word " turban" is, I imagine, derived from
the Turkish دلبند *dulbend,* or *durbend* as it is frequently pronounced by the common people.

we were enabled to see the great Padishah distinctly. His dress consisted of a very dark
green frock-coat with scarlet collar, cuffs,
and pocket flaps, richly embroidered in gold,
and having gold shoulder-straps; the overalls
were of the same colour, with gold stripes down
the seams; his black, European boots were
armed with brass spurs, and he wore, suspended by gold-embroidered cavalry slings, a
basket-hilted sword. On his head was a rich
red velvet fez, with an enormous and spread-
ing gold bullion tassel

This account of the dress bears, I am afraid,
a great resemblance to an extract from a military tailor's bill; but, as the lately-adopted
Frank uniform is not, certainly, an unimportant
feature in the new Turkish system, I have
imagined that, viewed in that light, these details might not be altogether without interest;
especially if we call to mind the wonderful dif-

ference that must have existed between the
times of Selim I., or of his son Suleyman I.
at the commencement of the sixteenth century,
and those of Mahmoud at the present day.

His majesty, notwithstanding that three or
four officers were sitting next to him, and ready
to do his bidding, supported over his head, and
with his own imperial hands, a rose-coloured
silk umbrella.

Sultan Mahmoud is decidedly a very handsome man : fine and intelligent black eyes,
good and manly features, a complexion which
tells more of the bivouac than of the luxurious effeminacy of the harem, great breadth of
shoulders, and a large open chest. Compared,
however, to the upper part of his figure, the
legs cannot be said to be in good proportion,
which is owing, as with respect to most of the
Turks, to the manner of sitting adopted by

them. His beard is one of the finest and
the blackest I ever saw.

On landing, he was received by a numerous
body of staff-officers; the band played the Sultan's march; the cannon of the adjoining forts,
as well as those of Asia, thundered forth the
roar of their artillery; the officers, inclining
themselves, shouted forth his titles and praises;
and the troops presented arms, and that in a
manner which pleased me much, for, whilst the
musket is held at the " present," by the left
hand, the right is brought up to the forehead
at the " salute," in the French manner. A
richly-caparisoned horse was in waiting, but
he did not mount, proceeding to the mosque
on foot, and preceded by priests burning in-
cense.

After remaining about twenty minutes at
his devotions, he re-embarked with the same

ceremonies, and pulled across to his beautiful villa on the opposite coast of Asia, whilst we quietly dropped down the stream to Top-khaneh, and from thence ascended to the house we had hired, situated on one side of the *Petit Champ des Morts*, and close to the Palace of England.

The fashionable promenade of the Perotes ran under our windows, and from these we enjoyed a very beautiful and extensive prospect, embracing the cemetery, Ters-khaneh, (the naval arsenal,) the dock-yards, the ships in commission anchored opposite, a long row of dismantled men-of-war along the quays, the Capudan pasha's palace above, the villages of Hassim Pasha, Piri Pasha, St. Demetrius, the Ok-Maidan, Ramas Chiftlek, Eyoub, the old walls near Constantine's palace, and the mosques of Muhammed, Selim, and Shah-zadeh. The house was, however, small and cold; and, with

the exception of divans, which in Turkish
houses supply in themselves alone, the place of
beds, chairs, and tables, totally unfurnished;
but this latter evil was most kindly remedied
by Sir Robert Gordon, who sent us, from his
palace, all we required, including that most
important and comfortable article, an English
stove; this, after much quarrelling with the
landlady, we had arranged much to our delight. As the generality of houses are built
of wood, and large districts of the town are
often, either through negligence or by incendia-
ries, burnt to the ground, the very idea of a
stove or fire-place, creates the greatest alarm
among the inhabitants, who use nothing but
manghals, or brasiers, over which are placed
tables covered with large cloths or blankets
reaching to the ground. The people sit
round these tables, with their knees over the

brasiers, and, as much of their persons covered
with the blanket as they can manage to con-
trive, and spend in this manner, in talking
scandal, the greater part of their days. I am
speaking of the Perotes and not of the Turks.
This table, with the blanket and charcoal fire,
forms the well-known *tendoor*.

We now lost no time in visiting the capital
of the Turkish empire, and, in fact, during our
whole stay at Pera, we scarcely ever allowed a
day to pass, at least when we were not otherwise engaged, that we did not go there, so much
were we pleased with it; and I think I may
safely say that I soon became as perfectly acquainted with the town as any Frank has ever
been, for I knew all the labyrinthine windings
of its numerous narrow streets and lanes better
than those of London or Naples. Many, however, are the residents of Pera who, after a so-

journ of many years, have never even once had the curiosity to cross the harbour, and a great many more who have been satisfied with one visit, and who look upon going to Istambool* as a journey replete with dangers and fatigue.

* This name is spelt استانبول, " Istanbool," but the *n* preceding the *b* is pronounced like *m*, as in amber for anber. Constantinople is also called by the Turks قسطنطينيه, " Kostantineah." Many are the derivations ascribed to the name Istambool ; some saying it is a mere corruption and abbreviation of Constantinople. The Greeks, led away by their vanity, absurdly deduce it from εἰς τὴν πολιν, " to the city ;" and again, others from اسلام بول, " a place abounding with the true faith ;" *i.e.* Muhammedanism ; and in this manner I have seen it spelt in several Turkish manuscripts—among others, in the Syahet Nameh of Evlia Efendi, which I have now before me. There is

Our wish being to see the Hippodrome on
our first visit, we embarked at Galata, and
landed at the Balik Iskeleh, or Fish-stairs,
passed by the Yeni Jamaa, (New Mosque,) and
then visited the tomb of Sultan Abd-ul-Hameed, the father of the present sovereign, and
of Sultan Mustafa.   Other members of the
family also repose here; the interior of this
turbeh, or sepulchral chapel, is very handsomely ornamented, chiefly with richly carved
and painted inscriptions from the Koran ; the
coffins, covered with rich cloths embroidered
with inscriptions, are ranged in the centre pa-
rallel to each other—those of the males being
distinguished by turbans.   From the ceiling
are suspended a great number of glass lamps of
different colours.

no doubt but that this latter is the correct origin of
the name.

Beyond this we saw the palace of the grand
vizir (or vizeer) Azem. The gate of this palace
has given the name of " the Sublime Porte" to
the Turkish government. By the people it is
indifferently called Dowlut Alieh, Babi Aaly,
Babi Saadet, and Pasha Kapoo. During the
late revolt of the Janizaries it was burnt down,
together with a great number of the adjoining
houses. The palace and gate are now rebuilt,
but the houses are still in ruins.

Passing under the walls of ancient Byzantium, which now enclose the seraglio, we came
to its grand entrance, called Bab Humayoon, a
large heavy building erected by Muhammed II.
It bears a long and intricate inscription, and
part of it says, " May God make the glory of
its master eternal!" On each side of the entrance is a niche in which are placed the heads
of culprits who have been executed. These

objects are, however, now rarely seen,—in fact, during the whole time I remained at Constantinople I never saw but one.*

In front of the gate is an open space, in the centre of which is a very beautiful marble fountain, richly carved, and ornamented with incriptions, arabesques, paint, and gilding; though smaller and less elaborately decorated than the one at Top-khaneh, it pleased me more. Ahmed III. erected it, and the verses which form the inscriptions, which are said to possess great beauty, are the composition of the Sultan himself.

On the right is the famous mosque of Aia

* I several times asked if they were not frequent; and the invariable answer (conveyed, I thought, in rather a tone of regret) was, " *Gechenlerdeh chok kerreh, shemdi seerek:*" " Formerly very often, now rarely."

Sofiya, built by Justinian on the ruins of a
chapel erected by Constantine the Great, and
converted into a mosque by Muhammed II., on
the very day of his triumphal entry into the
capital of the Greek empire. I was never enabled to enter it; for though foreign ambassadors, from long established custom, are entitled
to a firman, or order of admittance, yet from
some insulting and disrespectful conduct of a
Russian party, who spit on the carpets, and
otherwise ill-behaved themselves, just before I
arrived in Turkey, a polite note now accompa-
nies the demanded firman, in which the ambassador is requested not to avail himself of the
permission. The dome of this mosque is remarkable for its great depression, and com-
parative flatness; the exterior of the edifice is
far from beautiful, and its minarets are the
most clumsy and inelegant of any in the whole

city. Under the entrance porch are some
ancient porphyry columns, marble capitals,
&c.

Proceeding onwards, we entered the At-
Meidan, ات میدان, " the Plain of the Horse,"
or in other words, " the Race-course," (the
ancient Hippodrome,) an oblong, unpaved
square, one of whose lengths is occupied by the
beautiful mosque of Sultan Ahmed I,* called
also, from its being the only one which possesses six minarets, Alty Minarehler Jamaa.
On the opposite side is a barrack, a khan, and
the sultan's *ménagerie,* or the Arslan Khaneh ;
and at the lower end is the Darushifa, or Bimar
Khaneh, a lunatic asylum attached to the mosque.
In the area of the square are a granite obelisk,

* The *h* in this name, as in Mahmoud and others, is
hard and guttural ; Ahmed, therefore, is pronounced
Ahkmed.

another of marble, and a broken brazen pillar,
all standing on the *spina* of the Hippodrome,
which was doubtless adorned with many similar
objects, that perhaps might still be found by
removing the accumulated soil. The Egyptian
obelisk is of fine red Assouan granite; it is
sixty-two feet six inches in height, and bears
the following *cartouches* of the royal name
and titles.

Besides these, there are also other shields with
variations of the titles

From these it appears that this monument
was cut by order of Thothmes III.,* the sixth
sovereign of the eighteenth dynasty of the Pha-
raohs, and is probably one of those which were
originally erected at Karnak. With regard to
its date, we may, I think, state it at three thousand three hundred and sixty years back ; for
as the treaty entered into by Thothmes and the
Hyk-shos, 'or pastors, by which the latter
agreed to evacuate Egypt, was not signed till
1531 B.C., it is probable that the Egyptian king

* Thothmes III. was one of the Egyptian kings
who most distinguished himself by the erection of
splendid monuments.

was too much occupied with the war waged against the invaders of his country, to possess either the time or the means of erecting these stupendous monuments before that period—but we have every reason to believe that he commenced doing so immediately after.

The obelisk rests on four bronze blocks, bearing the marks of having had attached to them some figures or ornaments, probably the eagle with expanded wings. These blocks are placed on a white marble base, sculptured round with numerous figures representing some historical fact of the western empire, but the subject is obscure, the composition bad, and the execution worse. Under this again is another part of the pedestal, also of white marble, but of better workmanship, representing on one side the obelisk at the moment of its being raised in the Hippodrome, and on the other, when fixed on the *spina*, and the races taking place round it. On the side facing the *ménagerie* is the following inscription—

ΚΙΟΝΑΤΕΤΡΑΠΛΕΤΡΟΝΕΙΧΘΟΝΙΚΕΙΜΕΝΟΝΑΧΘΟΣ

ΜΟΝΟϹΑΝΑϹΤΗϹΑΟΘΕΙΔΟϹΙΟϹΒΑϹΙΛΕΤϹ

ΤΟΛΜΗϹΑϹΠΡΟΚΛΩΕΠΕΚΕΚΛΕΤΟΤΟϹΟϹΕϹΤΗ

ΚΙΩΝΗΛΙΟϹΕΝΖΙΑΚΟΝΤΑΔΤΟ

and on the side facing the mosque is another in Latin—

DIFICILIS QVONDAM DOMINIS PERERE SERENIS

IVSSVS   ET   EXTINCTIS   PALMAM   PORTARE
       TYRANNIS

OMNIA THEODOSIO CEDVNT SVBOLIQVE PE-
       RENNI

TER DENIS SIC VICTVS EGO DVOBVSQVE DIEBVS

IVDICE SVB PROCLO SVBLIME ELATVS AD AVRAS.

The lower lines of these inscriptions were

covered by the soil, which I was obliged to re-
move, and part of the last one was almost
effaced. The obelisk itself is not perfect,
part of the base having been broken or purposely cut off; it also inclines a little from
the perpendicular, leaning towards the *ménagerie*.

Gillius states, that close to the glass manufactory in the seraglio, there was another obelisk, but
that it was afterwards overthrown by an earthquake, and bought by Antonio Priuli, a Venetian nobleman, who proposed sending it to
Venice, to be placed in the Piazza San Stefano;
but I was unable to ascertain where it really is
at present. It was said to be thirty-five feet
long, and six feet square at the base. I have
seen a drawing, by Montfaucon, of an obelisk at
Constantinople, which, as it did not in the least
resemble the one just described, we may suppose

to have been meant to represent this lesser one : but at all events the signs which are marked upon it have no similitude to hieroglyphics.

At the end of the square stands another obelisk, its shaft not consisting, like that of the former, of one single block, but of eighty-three layers of stones, independent of the apex; and the whole was originally covered with plates of bronze fixed by cramps in holes which are still visible. This monument is in parts considerably injured, and the following inscription, which exists on the pedestal, cannot be deciphered without the greatest difficulty—

ΤΟΤΕΤΡΑΠΛΕΤΡΟΝΘΑΤΜΑΤΩΝΜΕΤΑΡCΙΩΝ

ΧΡΟΝΩΦΘΑΡΕΝΝΤΚΩΝΣΤΑΝΤΙΝΟΣΔΕΣΠΟΤΗΣ

ΟΡΟΜΑΝΟΤΠΑΙΣΔΟΞΑΤΗΣΣΚΗΠΤΟΤΧΙΑΣ

ΚΡΕΙΤΤΟΝΝΕΟΤΡΓΕΙΤΗΣΠΑΛΑΙΘΕΩΡΙΑΣ

ΟΓΑΡΚΟΛΟΞΞΟΞΟΘΑΜΒΟΞΗΝΞΝΤΗΡΟΔΩ

ΚΑΙΚΑΛΚΟΞΟΥΤΟΞΘΑΜΒΟΞΕΞΤΙΝΕΝΘΑΔΕ

The inscription does not exist at present in the entire state as given above; but the illegible parts are supplied from a copy I found in an old work.

The brazen pillar stands between these two obelisks, and is formed by three spirally entwined serpents, whose heads, branching out at the top, formerly supported a large golden patera. It was brought, together with many other valuable objects, from Delphi, by Constantine the Great. The heads no longer exist; one was severed, according to report, by a sabre-cut from Muhammed II., on the very day of his conquest of Constantinople; and the others were subsequently knocked off, and carried away by the orders of a Polish ambassador. Lady M. W. Montague, however, I believe,

mentions having seen one of them still connected with the body.—At present only about
eleven and a-half feet of the column are above-
ground.

During our visit to the At-Meidan, a battalion of the Nizam Jedeed, or New troops, were
going through their manœuvres; this was the
first time I had seen them working, and really,
considering the rawness of the materials, and
the short time they had been embodied, the
performance was very tolerable. The line,
which was formed three deep, was, when halted,
far from straight, but as soon as it advanced, it
became, to my surprise, very correctly dressed;
the coverings in column, the intervals, and the
wheelings, were very good, and certainly much
better than I had expected. The appearance
of the men was, however, far from being equally
satisfactory — the greater part consisting of

young, white-faced boys, and not the least attention seemed to be paid to placing them in
the ranks according to the gradations of their
heights; a boy of five feet was often seen
flanked by men of six, and *vice versâ*. The
uniform consisted of a blue short jacket without
skirts, red collar and cuff, blue Kossak overalls,
and black leather belts; the non-commissioned
officers wore side-arms. Many of the bayonets
were inlaid with gold. The words of command
were given with the French intonation.—But I
shall return hereafter to the subject of the
Turkish troops.

When the field-day was concluded, some of
the companies who were quartered close by
were dismissed. The men immediately flocked
round us, and expressed the greatest curiosity
at seeing me copying hieroglyphics, and Captain R. sketching a view of the Hippodrome;

and when my interpreter told them that I
understood what the characters meant, they all
wished to have them explained, and particularly
asked if they made mention of any concealed
treasure; to satisfy their curiosity I was obliged
to invent a story about a powerful sultan, and
the battles he had fought and gained, and
that to commemorate them this obelisk had
been raised.

Mustafa, my accompanying interpreter, was
a yasakji, (a rank next to that of ghawas,) a man
well known to all English travellers who have
been at Constantinople, Mr. Cartwright, the
consul-general, to whose service he is attached,
kindly allowing him to act as *cicerone* to stran-
gers. He is a native of Switzerland, and early
in life renounced Christianity for Islamism, and
served in Egypt and other campaigns; he
speaks English, French, Italian, German,

Arabic, and Turkish of course, and is extremely
useful; sometimes he also acts as Tartar in
inland excursions. He belonged to the forty-
second orta of Janizaries.

CHAPTER VIII.

The Bazaars — Eating-houses — Wine-shops — The
Burnt Pillar and other Columns—Therapia and its
vicinity— General Guilleminot—M. Jaubert—Visit
to the Sultan.

We generally crossed over at ten o'clock to
Constantinople, and walked about the bazaars
and bezesteens to make purchases, for during
the morning they are most crowded, and more
occurs and is seen to interest and amuse stran-
gers. At three o'clock they are shut, but even
before then, they are comparatively deserted.
About that time we usually entered some kabab
shop, of which there are many, very good and

clean, where we lunched on delicious mutton cut into small cubic pieces of half an inch square, roasted on little skewers, and having between them slices of artichokes, &c.; to this was added a small dish of salad, composed of a great variety of herbs, chopped fine. The beverage consisted of pure water or sherbet—I preferred the former; for notwithstanding its high renown, I must confess that " the blest sherbet, sublimed with snow," delights not me.

Those who wish for wine cannot obtain it in these houses, but must go to the regular wine-shops, where they will also generally be amused by some curious scenes, and where will be seen the dignified and apparently scrupulous Muhammedan, drinking off in succession large tumblers of wine, or more generally, glasses of ardent spirits, for there are many of them who draw a distinction between the impropriety of

drinking wine, and that of taking brandy, and
whilst they abstain from the former, hesitate
not to cheer themselves with the latter—asserting, that it cannot have been prohibited by
Muhammed, for the simple reason, that in his
days it was not known.   For the same reason,
also, neither champagne nor porter, (*arpa-su*,
or " barley-water,") are considered as prohibited.

At other times we lunched in the pastry-
cook shops; and though I am far from being an
amateur of cakes and sweet things, yet the
Turks are such proficients in this art, they
make such varieties, and are, moreover, so exceedingly clean in their manufacture of them,
(much more so than even in England or Holland,) that I was often led to commit great de-
vastation among the contents of the large
chrystal vases.   After thus restoring our

strength, we again sallied forth to view the different objects of interest in the town.

During our numerous walks, and in some of these we were alone, unaccompanied by either ghawas or yasakji, never did we experience the slightest insult; on the contrary, the generality of the people were markedly civil, often going into the middle of the street to make room for the Christian lady on the foot-path. It is true, that once or twice some women, prompted by more than ordinary curiosity, lifted up Lady Temple's veil to examine her features. This, however, was absolutely the only act we experienced which in the least bordered on rudeness;* and even these women, when they had satisfied their curiosity, and

* Once, indeed, a *Jew* made some insolent remark about us, for which conduct a Turk, who was standing by, felled him with a blow to the ground.

ascertained what sort of person a Frank woman really was, saluted us, and walked off, repeating some complimentary phrase, such as, " Peik," " Peik-guzel."

Not far from the At-Meidan, and on the summit of one of the seven hills, is the burnt pillar, or Yanmish-tash. It is formed of seven blocks of porphyry, the bottom of each piece projecting, and cut as a crown or wreath of laurel; this overlaps the block beneath and conceals the joint. There were formerly ten blocks, but three were overthrown by lightning, and their place supplied by twelve layers of white marble, round one of which is this inscription, stating the repairs to have been made by Manuel—

ΤΟΘΕΙΟΝΕΡΓΟΝΕΝΘΑΔΕΦΘΑΡΕΝΧΡΟΝΩΚΑΙΝΕΜΑΝΟΥΗΛΕΤ

ΣΕΒΗΣΑΥΤΟΚΡΑΤΩΡ.

On the pedestal existed, and, in fact, perhaps

still exists, under the coating of stone built
round the base by the Turks, another one thus
translated :—" Oh Christ ! Arbiter and Sovereign of the world, I address my prayer to
thee; protect this city, this sceptre, and the
Roman empire, and preserve them from all
dangers."

The column is ninety feet in height—its
pedestal twenty feet. It was brought from
Athens, and is said to be the work of Phidias.
On its capital originally stood a statue of
Apollo, which afterwards changed its name for
that of Constantine.   During the siege of Constantinople by the Turks, the Greeks fully expected, on the strength of an old prophecy,
that the angel of their salvation would appear
on its top, and drive out beyond the walls their
dreaded enemy with great slaughter, when he
should have reached this spot.   But—Muham-

med came—the angel did not—and the city belongs to the Turks.

The Yanmish-tash forms a very conspicuous object on approaching Estambool from the Propontis. The Adrianople street runs between it and an old ruined palace called the Elchi Khan, which, before the period when foreign ambassadors and ministers had taken up their residence at Pera, was appropriated for their use. It was originally established by the Christians, but after the conquest endowed by Ikbal Pasha.

There are three other columns within the walls of the city, namely, the Marcian, the Historical or Arcadian, and the Theodosian. The former, called by the Turks, Kiz-tash, or " the Maiden's Stone," stands on the heights overlooking the Yeni Baghcheh, near the street leading to the Edrineh Kapoo, and not far from tbe Serej-bazaar, or Saddle-market ; the vicinity is one vast scene of desolation, occasioned by fire, and the cannonade which took place during the late suppression of tbe Janizaries—the solid and high chimneys of whose barracks rise in different parts like the columns of some ruined temple.

The shaft of the Marcian column* is of grey granite, and the Corinthian capital, as well as the pedestal, is of white marble. On the summit is a sort of square white marble sarcophagus, with the Roman eagle at each of its corners. It is supposed to have contained Marcian's heart. The Turks, however, have a long story about a princess being kept there in order to avoid coming in contact with serpents, by the bite of one of which animals it had been prophesied she was to die; which

* Marcian died A.D. 456.

prediction, notwithstanding the precautions taken, they say, was verified, and point out the hole by which the serpent entered.* A nearly similar story is connected with the Kiz Koulleh, or Maiden's Tower, on the little island close to Scutari.

On the pedestal are two winged female figures, supporting a species of wheel, and this inscription, which was originally covered with bronze letters—

* Evliya Efendi, in his account of Constantinople, gives a somewhat different version of this story. He says, that near the Serej-bazaar, on the summit of a column which comes in contact with the heavens, is a chest of white marble, in which the unfortunate daughter of Sultan Puzenteen lies entombed; and that to protect her remains from ants and serpents, this column was made into a talisman.

PRINCIPIS HANC STATVAM MARCIANI

CERNI FORVMQVE

TER EJVS VOVIT QVOD TATIANVS

OPVS

Whether the statue stood on the summit of
the column, or only on the pedestal, and was
afterwards replaced by the column, is doubt-
ful. The whole of the monument has suffered
considerably from fire.

I think it is Tournefort who says, that the
discovery of this pillar does more honour to
Spon and Wheler, than to Tatianus, who erected
it. What is, however, meant by the discovery
of an erect and lofty column in a populous city,
it is not easy to understand.

The Arcadian column, called by the Turks
Dekili tash, or " the pyramidal stone," stands
near Jerrah Pasha Jamaa, in the district of

the Avret bazaar, or " market of women."*
It was erected by Arcadius in 405, A.D., after
the model of Trajan's at Rome.   The bas-reliefs, which spirally wound around it, represented that emperor's victories, and its height
was a hundred and forty-seven feet; but, at
present, nothing remains of it except the pedestal, the toro, and two or three feet of the
shaft, on which can still be distinguished a
chariot and a few figures.   It has suffered
greatly from fire and earthquakes; but the interior still exists; and within the pedestal are
three small chambers, on the ceiling of one of
which is the common monogram of our Sa-
viour's name, together with the letters A and Ω.

* This place derives its name, not from its being a
mart where female slaves are sold, but from having
been inhabited by that class of women who themselves dispose of their persons to any one who wishes
to possess them for a time.

The whole is of white marble, and some of the
blocks are of great size.

The Theodosian column is situated within
the precincts of the seraglio, and close to the
Selihtar-Agha's house.   Its height is about
fifty feet, and the shaft is composed either of
cipollino, or of white marble streaked with grey;
but which of the two I could not distinctly
ascertain, as the sea air has greatly discoloured
the stone.   The Corinthian capital is of white
marble, and not of *verde antico,* as stated by
some writers.   The pedestal is also of white
marble, but very coarsely cut; on it was this
inscription,

FORTVNAE REDVCI OB DEVICTOS GOTHOS

of which only the words REDVCI and DEVICTOS
GOTHOS are at present legible.

Some travellers have stated, but on what authority is not mentioned, that it also bore some Greek ones; but, though I searched carefully for them, I could not see the least vestige of any.

The following is a list of the principal public buildings, monuments, &c., which Constantinople contained during the time it was the capital of the western empire:—

5 Palaces,	2 Lusoria,
6 Domus divin. Augusti,	4 Cisterns,
3 Domus nobiliss.,	120 Pistrina priv.,
2 Senate Houses,	5 Granaries,
14 Churches,	153 Private baths,
2 Basilicas,	20 Pistrina publ.,
1 Augusteum,	5 Abattoirs,
1 Circus,	117 Gradus,
4 Forums,	2 Hollow columns,
2 Theatres,	1 Red column,
1 Capitol,	1 Colossus,
4 Nymphæa,	1 Golden tetrapylon,
52 Porticoes,	322 Streets,
1 Mint,	4388 Houses,
8 Public baths,	4 Harbours.

In this account, it will be observed that no
mention is made of either of the Egyptian obelisks; for the red pillar alludes to the Yanmish tash, and the Colossus is the obelisk covered with brass plates, which is still seen in
the At-Meidan. One of the hollow pillars is
the one called the Arcadian, the other no longer
exists. The tetrapylon must not be mistaken
for the tetrapleuron, the name by which the
" Colossus" is mentioned in the inscription
found on that monument. Nor can it meanthe
Porta Aurea, which had only three gates. It
must have been an edifice, I imagine, resembling the Arch of Janus at Rome.

On the 10th we rode to Therapia, where Sir
Robert Gordon had again asked us to spend
some days, and for which purpose he had sent
us his horses. The distance is about twelve
miles; and the road runs along the heights

which border the right shore of the Bosphorus, of whose waters we occasionally caught glimpses through the openings of the ravines which descend to them.

During our stay at Therapia, we made daily excursions to its beautiful environs. One of these was to Gul-dereh, " the valley of roses," which lies behind the village of Biuyuk-dereh, and which may be reached by a bridle-path. This valley takes its name from the plantations of roses which cover its surface, which, in the proper season, must form a lovely *coup d'œil*; and no doubt when all the flowers are in bloom, the sweetness of these rose-beds must make the air so fragrant, that the dew, before it falls on the earth, becomes changed into rosewater : so at least would an eastern poet say. When we rode through it, we could, however, scarcely discern the existence of any rose plants whatever; for, soon after the flowers have been gathered, the bushes are cut down to within a few inches of the ground. At the extremity of this valley, we ascended the steep hills on our left, passing by a pretty fountain, (the scene, in summer, of many parties of pleasure,) and then descended by an equally steep path to Biuyuk-dereh.*

Another time, we rowed across to the very pretty village of Kavak, passing by the stone quarries under the Giant's Mountain, the village, and the batteries of Yoro. On the summit of the steep hill which rises behind Kavak, and to which we ascended, stands an old castle built by the Genoese; its remains show it to have been of considerable extent, as the walls

* In the turfy plain near Biuyuk-dereh, is a remarkably large and beautiful tree, which forms the pride of the neighbourhood.

and outworks reached down to the water's edge. It was built on the site, and partly with the materials, of the temple of Serapis, and in its walls are found inserted fragments of columns, capitals, cornices, &c. The area of the castle is, at present, occupied by a Turkish village.

From a mound close to the castle, the view is extremely beautiful, embracing the Black sea, the *Symplegades*, or *Cyaneæ ins.*, (little rocky islets off the European shore under Fanaraki,* and called by the Franks *le Pavonare*,) the Bosphorus flowing from the Black Sea to Constantinople, the shores lined with batteries, villages, and gardens, another old castle

* The following, according to the generality of authorities, are the ancient and modern names of some of the spots along the banks of the Bosphorus:—Fanaraki, *Panium;* Feel boorun, *Coracium prom.;* Kecheli liman, *Pantichium sinus;* Maghara boorun,

on the opposite coast of Europe, and a fine
extent of hilly and wooded country on each
side.

> The wind swept down the Euxine, and the wave
> Broke foaming o'er the blue-Symplegades ;
> 'Tis a grand sight, from off " the Giant's grave"
> To watch the progress of those rolling seas
> Between the Bosphorus, as they lash and lave
> Europe and Asia. . . . . .

Byron is, however, wrong in saying that the
Symplegades are to be seen from the Giant's
Mountain, as such is not the case.

Proceeding on, we came to a remarkably
pretty and picturesque Turkish burial-ground,
embosomed in a plantation of oak trees. One

Argyronium prom. ; Kadlinje liman, *Cartacion sinus* ;
Kandeeli baghcheh, *Nicopolis* ; Koulleh baghcheh,
Cecrium ; Stavros, *Staurosis* ; Fanar baghcheh, *He-
ræum promontorium* ; Iskindar, or Scutari, *Chrysopolis* ; and Scutari Point, *Damalis*.

of the tomb-stones bore the imperial tooghra ;
but just as I was about to ascertain what distinguished ashes it covered, I was called away
by the shouts of the beaters ahead, who had
sprung a woodcock, and immediately after
by the report of Sir Robert's gun ; for, as
the whole country abounds with game, we
always carried our guns with us during our
rambles.   After making a tour through the
hills and valleys, we descended to the battery
of Yoro, where we entered the kaeek. Yoro
is the ancient *Hierom portus*, where formerly
existed a temple : but of this I found no ves-
tiges.

During another of our rambles, we crossed
the channel, landed at Unkhiar-iskelleh, walked
up the beautiful valley I have before noticed,
and ascended the sides of the Giant's Mountain, from whose summit we obtained another

magnificent view; bearing, however, a general
resemblance to the one from the Genoese castle.
It embraced the Bosphorus, the Mermereh-
deniz, the Kesheesh-daghy, or Mount Olympus,
and the Kara-deniz, or Black Sea. This mountain takes its name from the supposed tomb of
a giant, and certainly a giant of no ordinary
size; for, though it is asserted that only one
half of his body reposes on this spot, yet that
half alone measures fifty feet in length. According to the story told by the dervishes who
guard these remains, and who have a small
tekkeh here, this great man was no less a personage than Joshua the son of Nun, (بن نون
يوشع). Antiquarians are not, however, of ac-
cord with them on this point, some stating it
to be the tomb of Amycus, king of the Bebry-
ces, and others, the bed of Hercules.

Having reposed ourselves in a little adjoining *café*, and drank " the sober Mokah-berry's juice," we ascended, by another road, into a pretty valley, in which, at a place called Tokat, are the traces of a palace built by Suleyman the Magnificent.   Some large marble basins, into which bronze dragons still discharge clear streams of water, are all, however, that at present remain of its former splendor.

Most of these valleys, and the sides of the surrounding hills, were clothed with fine trees and shrubs, looking beautiful in their mellow and varied autumnal hues.

Between Therapia and Kefeli-keui, are the ruins of the convent of St. Euphemia, under which is a fountain, greatly venerated for its miraculous properties, of which many wonderful and romantic stories are related.

At Sir Robert Gordon's table, we made the acquaintance of the French ambassador, Gene-

ral Count Guilleminot, and his amiable family
—an acquaintance which, during our whole
residence at Stambool, gave us the greatest
pleasure. General Guilleminot is well known
in the military annals of his country. He entered the service in 1791, and soon after was
attached to the staff of Moreau, with whom he
contracted a most intimate friendship, so much
so indeed, as to render him, to a certain degree,
suspect in Napoleon's eyes. However, the emperor, aware of his talents and experience, employed him in the war of 1805 against Austria.
In 1807, he was named *Adjutant Commandant;*
entered Spain with the first army that marched
into that country, and much distinguished himself at Medina and Rio Secco in 1808 ; shortly
after, he was appointed general of brigade. In
the Russian campaign he gained fresh laurels,
especially at the battle of the Moskowa, and,

in the following year, gallantly repulsed the
Swedes at Dessau, for which he was promoted
to the rank of General of Division. In 1815,
he was appointed *Chef d'état Major* to an army
which was to be commanded by the Duke of
Berry against Napoleon; but, as both time and
soldiers were wanting, the army had no existence. He was one of the commissioners who
signed the capitulation of Paris. In 1823, he
followed the Duke of Angoulême into Spain,
and in fact commanded that army.

General Guilleminot is considered one of the
best officers in the French service; and his
reputation, as a man of honour and a friend to
liberty, is not inferior to that which he has
gained as a soldier.

We also met Monsieur Amédée Jaubert,
Conseiller d'Ambassade, one of the best oriental scholars of the present day, and well known

for his works, his travels, and his lectures. He
was Napoleon's oriental secretary, and filled
many important diplomatic missions to the
Sublime Porte, and to the Shah of Persia. He
it was that brought over to France from
Thibet, the famous goats, from whose hair the
renowned Kushmeer shalls are made. In April,
1815, the emperor sent him to Constantinople
as minister extraordinary to the sultan. He
entered the palace occupied by the minister of
Louis XVIII., and displaying, together with
his suite, the tricoloured cockade, the example
was immediately followed by most of the French
mission and French merchants. Having sub-
stituted over the gates of the palace, the proud,
imperial eagle of Napoleon, for the pale lilies
of the Bourbons, the Turkish ministry begged
that the latter might be restored. M. Jaubert
refused; on which a detachment of Janizaries

were ordered to take down the eagles of the empire. Had the battle of Waterloo met with a different result, it is probable that the vizeer would have suffered for not having been sufficiently clear-sighted to choose the proper line of policy.

M. Jaubert is an active, brave, and intelligent man, and quite adapted to the perilous missions with which he was entrusted by Napoleon.

We visited the sultan's stables to see the lately-arrived giraffe,* the same that we had met in the Dardanelles. It is the largest of the species hitherto imported into Europe, measuring to the summit of the head nearly fifteen feet in height. It appeared in bad condition,

* This animal is called by the Turks, *Zurnapa,* سرناپا, and by the Arabs, ظريف, Dzareef, " the graceful," or " the elegant."

being, from the effects of its long voyage, both thin and ragged.

Only three of the horses from Egypt were at Therapia, the rest having been left at Stambool; but we saw about a hundred and sixty others—Turkish, Arabians, Egyptians, Dongolese, Syrian, and Turkoman. Few, however, judging from appearance, seemed possessed of any very transcendant qualities, or remarkable beauty, though we were told that they were all good at work.

The Turkish horses are easily distinguished from others by their forms. They have good middle pieces though rather round; high and thick crests resembling in their immense arch that of the Godolphin Arabian. Their heads are rather coarse and badly put on; and their legs are short, flat, and bony. The favourite colours are the pie-balds and the strawberries,

especially when the two near legs and one of
the off ones are white.   The Italians have the
same predilection, saying, *Balzano a tre, è ca-
vallo di Rè*.   Whitemuzzles and wall-eyes are
also considered as great beauties.

One horse was particularly pointed out to us
as remarkable for his extraordinary colour,
which was certainly most singular, being a
perfectly bright crimson shade of chesnut,
which, viewed under the influence of the sun's
rays, looked exactly like the finest carmine.   I.
imagined it to be produced by the khennah, or
some other dye, but was positively assured it
was the horse's natural colour.

The Dongolese horses are excellently adapted
for the carriage, many being from sixteen to
seventeen hands high, very showy, and with
grand action.   They are, however, remarkably
long in the back, and rough in their movements
when rode.

Sadih Khan, a Persian who has long resided in England, had lately arrived at Constantinople from his own country, bringing with him, amongst other horses, one of the breed of Takkah in Khorassan, which, in common with all his race, was possessed of the curious distinction of having no mane. He was altogether a showy horse, with an English thorough-bred look about him.

The horses in Turkey are all kept excessively fat, and are shod with bar shoes, with high projecting nail-heads, there being no groove.

On Friday I again went, with three English officers of the eighteenth regiment of infantry, (who were lately arrived from Corfu on a shooting excursion,) to see the sultan going to mosque. He generally goes to a different place of worship every week—this day he chose Yali-keui in Asia. The ceremonies were the same as what we had

before seen, but his dress was different, resembling exactly the *petite tenue* of our
third light dragoons. After leaving the mosque
he mounted his horse, and rode to the turfy
valley of Unkhiar-iskelleh, where he amused
himself by galloping about, and showing off
his powers of equitation. He possesses a very
firm and graceful seat, and has apparently a
good and light bridle-hand. He rode with long
stirrup-leathers, like ourselves. His horse appointments were very rich and splendid, and
decorated with pearls and precious stones. I
was told that he well understands cavalry manœuvres, and often delights in putting his
squadrons through a field-day. His instructor
was Captain Calosso, a Piedmontese officer, at
present instructor-general of the Turkish cavalry, with the rank of colonel.

On the following day, the 13th, I accom-

panied our ambassador, who had demanded a
private audience with the sultan for the purpose of delivering his credentials from William
IV. I was very sensible of Sir Robert Gordon's kindness on this occasion, for in order to
obtain permission for me to go with him, he
had to undertake a long and very troublesome
correspondence with the Reis Efendi. Every
thing being at last arranged, and it being at the
same time understood that this deviation from
the established etiquette of the court was not
to serve as a precedent—for no Frank subjects
are permitted to approach the sultan, except
when a new ambassador or minister has, on his
arrival, an audience of introduction, on which
occasion the subjects of that minister's sovereign
are allowed to follow in his *suite*—we embarked in the ambassador's state kaeek, pulled
by fourteen oars. As aide-de-camp to Sir

Robert Gordon I put on my full-dress uniform of hussars. Mr. Villiers carried the king's letter, enclosed in a rich portefeuille of gold and silver tissue. M. Chabert, chief dragoman* of the embassy, was in the very handsome oriental full-dress of his office, as were also the pilot, ghawases, and servants. The sailors were dressed in green velvet jackets embroidered with gold, whilst the silken flag of England waved from the prow.

On landing at the stairs of the imperial serai the ambassador was received by the troops with presented arms, and we were then ushered into an apartment on the ground-floor, where we found the Reis Efendi, Ahmed Hameed Bey,† attended by his dragoman, Esrar Efendi.

---

* A word corrupted from ترجمان, *terjeman,* " an interpreter."

† Called also, from having six fingers on one of his hands, Alty-Parmak Pasha.

The Reis Efendi is a very short little man with a dark-grey beard, and, with the exception of sharp and penetrating eyes, possessing a look the reverse of *distingué*. The dragoman was a person of most diminutive stature. They were both covered from the neck to the feet with dark and unornamented cloaks, and wore on their heads the simple red fez.

Shortly after, Mustafa Efendi, the sultan's private secretary and favourite, entered the room followed by Ahmed Fethi, pasha of the Bosphorus and colonel-in-chief of the guards,* and another officer.

Mustafa is a good-looking fat young man, and Ahmed has a pleasing and soldier-like appearance. They were both dressed in a dark

* The rank of Pasha of the Bosphorus and colonel of the guards, unites the charges and duties of the Ex-Bostanji Bashi.

blue uniform with scarlet facings. The latter spoke a little French.

Next entered the Serasker, (سرعسكر "head of the army,") Hosrew Mehemmed Pasha, a jovial and good-looking old man with a beard of snowy whiteness;* but, notwithstanding his jovial, good-natured, and *bon enfant* looks, he is said to be very sanguinary and cruel. " Is it possible," I asked, " that so amiable a looking man did really cut off so many heads?" " *Her goon,*"—" every day," was the answer.

With the exception of the Reis Efendi, who was seated on the divan, the rest of the party occupied chairs, but the old habit of crossing their legs seemed not to have quite abandoned them, for they tucked them up as much as possible, by resting them on the bars beneath.

* For a list of the different cabinet ministers, and other officers of the Sublime Porte, see Appendix.

Pipes and coffee were served, the latter quite in the Frank manner, with saucers, spoons, sugar, and even sugar-tongs. We remained here about an hour, conversing on a variety of subjects, but all far from having a serious tendency—women, and affairs of gallantry, being the themes most dwelt upon. The Serasker and Mustafa were particularly gay, cutting jokes, and laughing loud and freely. At last we were summoned up-stairs to the imperial presence.

Passing through several rooms, furnished not only with the usual divans, but with several articles of Frank furniture, such as consoles, ormolu clocks, Sevre vases with artificial flowers, pier-glasses, and pictures, we entered a room overlooking the waters of the Bosphorus, and there, seated on a divan, we beheld the mighty lord of the Othman empire, Ghazi Sultaun

Mahmoud Khan Aadli — محمود خان عدلی
غازی سلطان, " the Victorious Sultan Mahmoud,
Khan, the Just."* Khan is the old Turkoman
title.

* Sultan Mahmoud, born 20th July, 1785, is the son
of Sultan Abd-al-Hameed, and nephew of Sultan Selim
III. He succeeded his brother, Sultan Mustafa IV.,
on the 28th July 1808. He has several daughters,
but only two sons, Abd-al-Mesheed, born 1823, and
Abd-al-Azeez, born February, 1830. His eldest daughter, Saleehah, born 1811, it is said, is to be married
to Haleel, Capudan Pasha.

In the Appendix I have inserted his lineage traced
from Adam! I copied it from a very handsome
Turkish manuscript, which was, however, partly effaced, as will be seen from the three blanks, where
the names were perfectly illegible. The Turks, and
all eastern nations, have, at all times, been very particular in keeping correct genealogical tables, not only
of themselves but also of their horses.

He was dressed in the same uniform he wore
when I saw him at Yeni-Keui, and on his left
breast wore a magnificent decoration in diamonds and rubies, representing the crescent, the
star, and a plume of feathers arranged like
those which form the distinguishing mark of a
Prince of Wales. The room was very simply
furnished; the only ornaments it bore were his
arms suspended from the wall; his sabre, pistols,
and topuz, were mounted in gold, and studded
with diamonds, sapphires, rubies, and emeralds.
Sir Robert Gordon addressed him in French,
and his speech was immediately translated into
Turkish by Esrar Efendi. The sultan then returned his answer in Turkish, which was translated into French by M. Chabert.

On commencing his speech, which was of considerable length, the sultan seemed rather nervous, but his voice soon recovered its firmness.

His delivery was excellent, and quite oratorical, and, as I afterwards heard, his words were well chosen, and his sentences well turned. In fact, he has paid great attention to literature, and is deeply read, not only in the Turkish, but also in the Arabic and Persian languages, and is moreover a very tolerable poet. His expressions bore witness to his great friendship for our king and the English nation, and were excessively complimentary and kind to Sir Robert Gordon personally. After this he desired that Mr. Villiers and myself should be presented to him, when, through the dragoman, he asked me how I liked those parts of his dominions which I had visited, and when, in answering this question, I said, that I had been delighted with all I had seen, I spoke not in the matter-of-course and complimentary manner, but really as I felt. Sir Robert Gordon then added that I was

very anxious to see some reviews of the new
troops, to which his Highness answered " Insh'
allah, when I return to Stambool he shall see
plenty ;" and at the same time ordered Ahmed
Pasha to afford me every facility in seeing the
different barracks, and the interior economy of
the troops.

After talking some time longer with the ambassador, during which time he was not only
very affable, but even gay, we bowed, and
reined back out of the room, (where we had
remained about half an hour,) and returned to
the apartment where we had first been received.
Here we again smoked the delicious weed of
Jebeleh, drank amber-perfumed Mokah coffee,
and sipped sherbets of the violet (the best,) the
white rose, the red rose, the carnation, and a
variety of other flowers, all served in richly
cut crystal vases, with gold covers. Before our

departure, Mustafa Efendi had his best horses paraded in the garden, and close to the windows, for our inspection.

Most Turkish houses have some sentence from the Koran painted on the façade; the words inscribed both on the outside of the sultan's serai, and in the rooms, were حا يظ *(Ya Hafiz !)* " Oh Protector !"

On Sunday we returned to town by water.

CHAPTER IX.

Remains of Old Byzantium—Ancient Cisterns—Aqueduct of Valens—Principal Mosques—The Suleymanieh—Tombs of the Suleymans—Benevolent Institutions—Universities—Lunatic Asylum.

On returning to Stambool, we recommenced our search after the remains of old Byzantium.

According to the list of buildings and monuments given a few pages back, it appears that there were four sets of public cisterns. Gillius, however, if I mistake not, increases the number to six; there are but two at present, which

are still well preserved; namely, one near the
Yanmish tash, called by the Turks, Bin-
bir-deerek, (the thousand and one pillars,)
Yerabatan Serai, and Eer Ewi, (subterranean
palace;) and another near Santa Sofia, called
Batan Serai. The former is used as a place
for spinning silk: the entrance to it is a little
lower than the level of the capitals which sup-
port the vault, and a wooden staircase leads to
the bottom.

The size of this cistern, and the number of
pillars it contains, has afforded incessant subject of dispute—no two persons, I believe, being
agreed on the point; but this may easily be
accounted for by the fact, that the Turks,
whose houses are situated round it, from time
to time have enclosed parts of it for the purpose of making cellars and store-rooms. Some
writers have stated the number to be two hun-

dred and twelve; others, three hundred and sixty-six; and others again, by considering them as double ones, at four hundred and twenty-four. They are called double, from the shaft of the columns having, half way up their length, a false pedestal, up to which the water was allowed to mount, so that the upper half of the columns seemed to rest with these pedestals on the surface of the water.

Dr. Walsh, however, gives a still grander account of this reservoir, describing it as " an arched roof supported by six hundred and seventy-two marble columns, each column consisting of *three*, standing on the top of each other."

As I did not myself count them, I cannot decide which of these statements is correct, though I must confess that I certainly did not see the treble order. There is, how-

ever, no reason, after all, why there may not
still exist even as many as the one thousand
and one, a portion, as I before observed, being
inclosed within the walls.

Some of the capitals were evidently taken
from the materials of other edifices; but the
generality of them are simply square blocks of
stone with the edges rounded off: this cistern
is supposed to have been that of Philoxenus.
Andreossi asserts, that it was capable of containing a sufficiency of water to meet the de-
mands of the city for sixty days: within its
area are two wells of good water.

The soil has so much accumulated, that it
reaches to within five or six feet of the middle
pedestals.

The other cistern, called formerly *Cisterna
Basilica*, is situated under a house in a street
near Aya Sofiya Jamaa. Those who wish to

see it must ask permission from the Turk who owns this house. Descending into a garden which occupies a part of the cistern where the vault has fallen in, he sees a sort of archway, entering which a forest of columns bursts on the sight. The part of the reservoir which is vaulted over, and on which part of the town is built, is in very good preservation, and still serves the purpose for which it was originally constructed; and numbers of pipes, or pump-tubes, are seen descending into the water it contains, in all directions, from the houses above.

Here again I was unable to ascertain the exact number of columns for want of a boat, the one which is generally kept there being under repair. Gillius states that he counted three hundred and thirty-six. It however seemed to be of very great extent, long rows

of columns continuing to a considerable distance, and then becoming gradually lost to
the eye, in the darkness of the opposite extremity. The Turks say that it reaches as
far as the At-Meidan. The columns are of
different forms and dimensions, some representing the trunks of trees, others fluted, and
many quite plain, whilst the capitals vary
from the rich Corinthian to plain square blocks.
In the water I observed a great number of fish,
which seemed quite tame, in consequence of
being regularly fed by the Turk.

This visit of mine caused great alarm in the
household; the master was absent, and upon
entering we found ourselves in the midst of his
female slaves, some of them working, others
playing in the *hauli*, (the hall or interior court,)
who, on seeing us, all ran screaming to the
harem, covering their faces with their hands;

a small negro boy alone remaining, who acted as *cicerone.*

The aqueduct of Valens, or as it is now called, the Bosjohan Kemeri, forms a very conspicuous feature in the picture of Constantinople. In many parts it has two tiers of arches, and is of considerable breadth, having on its summit a convenient path, which connects, without descending into the intermediate valley, two districts of the town. It is chiefly built of stone, but in parts is intermixed with brick-work. Some of the arches (which span different streets) would form very picturesque sketches, being adorned with ivy and festooning creepers, besides large shrubs, whose roots are fixed in the interstices of the stones. This aqueduct underwent a complete repair in the reign of Suleyman I., and in fact, was in many parts completely rebuilt by him.

One day, whilst sketching this building, we were startled by a sudden crash of wild discordant music and song ;* and on proceeding to ascertain the cause, we discovered a house surrounded by musicians, and other persons bearing a litter covered with feathers, plumes, and flags ;—a hajji had just reached his home after making the long and perilous pilgrimage to Mekkah.

With the exception of the *Porta Aurea*, and the city walls, of which I shall speak hereafter, the above-mentioned edifices and monuments form the only considerable ruins of ancient Byzantium.

I shall now briefly notice some of the mosques —the principal structures erected by the Turks. Of these there are a considerable number ; the most remarkable (I place them chro-

* See specimens of Turkish love songs in Appendix.

nologically) are,—1. Aya Sofiya, the famous
Christian shrine, converted into a mosque by
Muhammed II. on the day of his capture of
Constantinople; 2. Sultan Mehemmed, erected
by Muhammed II. 3. Eyoob, by Muhammed II. 4. Sultan Bayazeed, by Bayazeed II.
5. Sultan Selim, commenced by Selim I., and
completed by his son, Suleyman I. 6. Shah-
zadeh, by Suleyman I. 7. Sultan Suleyman,
or Suleymanieh, by Suleyman I. 8. Sultan
Ahmed, by Ahmed I. 9. Noor-Othmanieh,
commenced by Mahmood I., and finished by
Othman III. 10. Yeni Jamaa, by the Valideh Terkhann Sultana, the wife of Ibrahim I.,
and mother of Muhammed IV. 11. Valideh
Jamaa, by Rabieh Gulnoosh Sultana, wife of
Muhammed IV., and mother of Mustafa II.
and Ahmed II. 12. Laléhli, by Mustafa III.
13. Aiazma Jamaa, by Mustafa III.; and

I also sent a message to one of the priests,
stating how thankful I should feel if he would
show me the different beauties of the edifice.
Accordingly, at the appointed hour we met
him at the entrance, left, of course, our boots
and shoes at the door, (which, by the bye, could
not be done in a Christian country, at least if
the owners should entertain the wish of seeing
them again,) and passing through a beautiful
gate, entered the holy fane, and certainly never
was I struck with more serious and devotional
feelings. The building is of vast extent, lofty,
and wide—no glaring and dazzling ornaments
like those in Catholic churches meet the eye,
nor is it offended by Smithfield-pens, for to nothing else can I compare the pews which deco-
rate our churches at home; the whole space is
open, and the marble floor is covered with the
soft carpets of Persia, over which, slowly and

silently, the pious Moslem bends his way to some favourite corner. A number of small windows fitted with coloured glass, admit a sober and mellow light, and give, if I may use the expression, a religious air to the interior, preventing the mind from being distracted or diverted by the glitter of ornaments and decorations.

This mosque was built in 691 of the Hejrah (1554) by the architect Sinan, and finished two years after, chiefly with materials taken from the church of St. Euphemia, at Kadi-keui, the ancient *Chalcedon*. Some Turkish authors, however, state its construction to have occupied a longer period, asserting that the first stone was laid in Jamadi-awal 957, and that the edifice was not *completely* finished till Zil-hijjeh 964. It cost seventy-four million three hundred thousand piastres.

The dome is very handsome and bold, and rests on four enormous piers, besides four Egyptian columns of red granite, sixty feet high, each of one single block, and brought from Kahira as a present, by Karinjeh Capudan. It is covered with bronze, and is flanked by two half-domes. From the dome are suspended a vast number of small glass lamps of different colours, which reach to about six or seven feet from the floor; they are said by Muhammedan writers to have been originally twenty-two thousand in number.

Long inscriptions in the beautiful intricacies of the elegant Soolssi and Guzafi characters, generally in gold relief, on a *lapis lazuli* coloured ground, adorn different parts of the walls. The grand altar, which fronts the principal entrance, is extremely simple; above it is a window of coloured glass, and on each side

two gigantic wax candles, measuring no less
than fifteen feet in height and five in circumference, and said to weigh twenty cantars. On
the left of the altar, or mihrab, is the minber,
an elevated pulpit, with a narrow and steep
flight of marble steps leading to it. In other
parts of the mosque are three oblong-square
galleries, or mahfils, resting on a number of
little marble columns, inlaid with rich mosaic
work, like those seen at Salerno, and Ravella,
and in other parts of the Neapolitan territories,
and which are called Saracenic. One of these
galleries belongs to the sultan, and is surrounded by gilt lattice-work—another is of
some scarce wood inlaid with mother-of-pearl.

In front of the principal entrance is an open
court, with a beautiful fountain in the centre,
and a covered cloister, or gallery, running
round it; this gallery has twenty-seven little
domes, and is supported by twenty-four beauti-

ful columns of verd' antico, porphyry, granite, and marble, whose pedestals are of bronze.

In rear of the mosque are the *turbehs*, or tombs of Suleyman and his well-known wife, the famous Roxelana, called in Turkish, Hessiah. Suleyman's turbeh is a handsome octagonal chapel, surmounted by a dome; round the lower half of the building runs a covered projecting gallery, supported by double rows of verd' antico columns; the edifice itself is of white marble, with borders and labels of rose-colour. In the interior are eight verd' antico pillars, one in each corner; the walls are decorated with inscriptions in yellow letters on a blue field, and the dome, (from which are suspended many lamps kept burning night and day,) is of richly carved cedar-wood, inlaid with mother-of-pearl, and studded, according to the account of the turbehdar, with diamonds, rubies, and pearls.

There are six coffins in all, three of males, namely, Suleyman I., Suleyman II., son of Ibrahim, and Ahmed II., also son of Ibrahim, and three of females; the bodies are not, however, in the coffins, but are buried in the earth under them. The cenotaphs of the princes are surrounded with wooden railings inlaid with mother-of-pearl, and covered with rich silks, embroidered with Arabic sentences, being veils which have surrounded the prophet's tomb at Medinah.* At the head of each are the imperial turbans with the zulfs or aigrettes worn by the sultans—but Suleyman's turban is preserved in a little closet.

* These veils are renewed by each sultan on his accession to the throne ; and, whenever the former ones become worn out. The old ones are taken back to Constantinople, and are used to cover the tombs of the sultans.

We also see a model of the sacred temple of
Mekkah, together with the adjoining mountain
and valley; and a number of handsome copies
of the Koran are kept for the use of the pious.
Service is still regularly performed in this
chapel; twelve readers are also appointed, who
are paid to read extracts from the Koran, to
any person who desires them; six turbehdars
are maintained to keep the place in order.

Suleyman having died whilst fighting the
Christians, at the siege of Zieghet, in 974
Hejra (A.D. 1566) is considered as a sheheed, or
martyr. At his funeral the Namaz was performed over his body according to the rules of
the Imam Shafi, which he had observed during
his life; in fact, he was always accompanied
by Imam Nakybul Eshref, one of the sect.
After this the clergy were ordered to finish the
Telaveti Koran forty times a day, for forty
consecutive days.

Suleyman was surnamed *Kanooni*, " the
Legislator ;" another derivation is given of this
word in the recently-published " Journal of a
Nobleman," in which it is seriously stated that
he was " surnamed Kanouny, for having introduced the use of *cannon* in Turkey."

The above-mentioned turbehs stand in a
garden, and, with the mosque, occupy a level
space on the summit of one of the seven hills,
and are surrounded by a wall and an avenue of
trees. From this elevated terrace is obtained
a fine view of the town, Galata, Pera, Scutari,
and the Bosphorus. Outside the square are
hospitals, schools, libraries, and lunatic asylums, and the residence of the Sheikh ul
Islam, formerly the palace of the Janizary
Agha; on the left side runs a long row of
cafés, formerly resorted to by opium-eaters,
but at present almost deserted.

To most of the mosques, as well as to this of Suleyman, are attached a number of useful and benevolent establishments—such as imarets, (*hospices,*) where the priests and the poor are fed ; taby khanehs and bimar khanehs, (lunatic asylums and hospitals;) mektebs, (schools ;) mudressehs, (colleges ;) and ketab khanehs, (or libraries.)

One of the first acts of Muhammed II., after his conquest of Constantinople, was that of founding two universities,—the one attached to Aya Sofiya, the other to the Muhammedeah ; the first contained six colleges, the latter sixteen, and the most talented men in the empire were appointed as teachers. The Muhammedeah is still considered as one of the chief boasts of the Constantinopolitans. There are more than five hundred mudressehs, each bearing the name of its founder; a great

number of mektebs, and thirty public libraries,
independent of the one in the seraglio.

Muhammed II. wished that the new mosque
he proposed building, which was to bear his
own name, should rival that of Aya Sofiyah, and
for this purpose had collected a number of
splendid columns, and other rare materials.
His architect, however, to render the building
stronger, shortened these columns by three
cubits.   This naturally greatly enraged the
sultan, who ordered the architect's hands to be
cut off.   Evlia Efendi, who mentions this fact
in his Syahet Nameh, adds a curious anecdote
connected with this affair.   He states that the
architect summoned the sultan to appear before
a court of law to answer for his conduct.   Muhammed obeyed the summons; when, after the
plaintiff and defendant had been heard, the
Islambol-molassi sentenced the sultan to pay

a daily sum of ten akchehs to the architect, in compensation for the loss of his hands. Muhammed doubled the sum, to the great delight of the plaintiff, who professed himself perfectly satisfied. This shows the great difference in the value of money at that time to what it is at present, unless we choose to account for it by the small value in which hands were then held.*

Every mosque is possessed of considerable revenues; that of the Suleymanieh amounted to twenty-five thousand piastres, and that of Aya Sofiya to one million; very large sums, when

* Three akchehs make one para, forty paras one piastre, and, calculating at the present rate of exchange, (seventy-seven,) the twenty akchehs would now only equal the four hundred and fifty-sixth part of one pound sterling, or a little more than a halfpenny a day.

we recollect that the piastre, at that time, was perhaps nearly equal to the Spanish dollar. The expenses have never exceeded the half, or, at most, two-thirds of these revenues.

We visited, among other establishments, the lunatic asylum attached to the Suleymanieh. It consists of two open courts, round which run covered galleries, and into these the cells open : the doors are left open, and any one may enter ; the patients are chained, and generally occupy the deep recesses of the grated windows which look into the court. The unfortunate beings are allowed a bed and two blankets ; but they must, notwithstanding, suffer greatly from the cold in winter : few of them were very furious, but all begged for tobacco.

According to a work published in 1827 on insanity, by order of the French government, it appears that no less than seven hundred and

fifty-five tailors were confined at Paris in the
Salpêtrière alone, and that, on an average,
there are two hundred and eighty-five mad
tailors in every thousand.   Many medical men
have attributed this great proportion to the
sedentary position adopted by this class of persons; and it would be curious to ascertain,
whether the Turks and other eastern nations,
who sit in the same attitude during the greater
part of the day, are, more than other people,
subject to this dreadful affliction; though, considering the case in another point of view, they
ought undoubtedly to be exempt from it, as
they always keep their *heads shaved.*

Not only the sultans and pashas, but private
individuals generally leave a part of their fortunes towards supporting the different benevolent institutions already established, and also,
when their means are sufficient for the purpose,
for founding new ones.   We must certainly look

upon the Turks as a nation possessed of much charitable feeling, which they exercise in its purity, uncontaminated by any germ of vanity or ostentation; for by far the greater number of the fountains erected in the desart bear no inscription to commemorate their founder; and hosts of unclean and abhorred dogs who possess no master, are daily fed by the charitable Turks. The piety also of the Moslem seems sincere: often have I stopped to admire them at their prayers, when they seem to be so entirely wrapped up in their devotion as to be perfectly unconscious of the bustle of the surrounding scene: no false shame prevents them, at the stated hours appointed for prayer, from kneeling down in the camp, at the road side, or in the crowded street; nor do they omit doing so in the midst of vast solitudes, where they cannot be aware that any eye but that of the Almighty is bent on them.

The Koran is certainly a fine code of mo-
rals; and, when freed from the interpretations
and false constructions of fanatic followers, in-
culcates much greater toleration, and more li-
berality, than we are generally inclined to con-
cede to it.   Among other instances, I shall
quote the seventy-fourth verse of the fifth
chapter, called " the table." — It is as follows :—

" For those who have believed, and those
who have been Jews, and the Christians, and
the Sabeans, every man who has believed in
God, and in the day of resurrection, and who
has performed good works, all these will meet
their reward from the Lord."*   The ex-

* As I am but a very indifferent Arabic scholar, I
insert the original :

الى الدين هادوا و النصاري و الصابيين
من امن بالله و ايوم الاخر عمل صالا
عند ربهم فلهم اجرهم

pounders of our religion do not certainly speak thus: where, for example, can we find any-thing to match

> . . . . Athanasius' curse,
> Which doth your true believer so much please,
> And decorates the book of Common Prayer?

I have somewhere read the following account of the Muhammedan religion, which seems drawn up with considerable fairness.—The Muhammedans are neither atheists nor idolators. On the contrary, their religion, false as it is, has many points in common with the true one. They believe in one God Almighty, Creator of all, just and merciful; they abhor polytheism and idolatry; they hold the immortality of the soul, a final judgment, a heaven, a hell, angels good and bad, and even guardian angels; they ac-knowledge a universal deluge; they honour the patriarch Abraham as the father and first au-

G 2

thor of their religion; they hold Moses and
Christ to have been great prophets sent from
God, and the law and the Gospel to be sacred
books. In contrast with the corrupt system
which it has displaced, it has, in many respects,
the advantage; nay, it may be said to have
embodied more truth and less error than the
Romish superstition in its vulgar form. Sa-
ladin's was a more Christian faith than that of
Cœur de Lion, and Mekkah is the scene of
a purer worship than Rome. Wherever Muhammedanism spread, it expelled idolatry; the
Christianity of Rome adopted and perpetuated
it. The Moslems denounced, and sometimes
extirpated image worshippers; but the ortho-
dox, on the plea of heresy, destroyed their
brethren. The religion of the Koran, sensual
as are the future rewards it holds out to the
faithful, is more spiritual than that which

dealt in absolution and indulgences: the former at least postpones the gratification of the passions to a future state, while the latter let them loose in this.   Nor were the pretensions of Muhammed more impious than those of the pope. The Arabian impostor promised paradise to the faithful, the Roman pontiff sold heaven to the highest bidder, and fixed a price on the pains of hell.   The morality of the Koran is also far purer than that of the canons; and finally, the devotion of the mosque has brought the Moslem into a more intimate communion with the idea of Deity, and partakes more of the character of worship than the unmeaning ceremonials of the Romish church.   In Spain the two systems came fairly into opposition.

But enough of this, for I had designed only a slight sketch of Constantinople—not an essay on the merits or demerits of the Moslem creed.

It must, however, literally confine itself to the
character of a sketch, for it would be in vain
for me to undertake a full description of its
beauties, or to call up the vast multitude of
events connected with its history, which render
it, in the eyes of all, one of the most interesting
spots on earth ; besides which, the pens of so
many eloquent writers have been employed to
sing its praises, that my cursory observations,
at random strung, can scarce, I fear, merit the
name even of a sketch.

Some of these accounts are very curious.
Ibn Batuta, (a Moslem,) after representing
himself as being much pleased with Constantinople, chimes in with the prophetic wish of
El Harawi, a writer of the thirteenth century,
who exclaims, " This city, which is greater
than its fame, may God of his bounty and
grace, make the capital of Islamism !" Little

did he imagine how soon his wishes would be fulfilled.

I was much struck with a passage in the travels of Ibn Batuta, who states that he was prevented from visiting St. Sophia, " as a great number of crosses were placed on and around it, to exclude the infidels." What a number of thoughts are called up by this one short sentence !

CHAPTER X.

The Army—The Nizam Jedeed—Cavalry—Uniform—
Manœuvres—Colonel Calosso—Barracks—Infantry
—Artillery—Military Hospitals—Russia and Turkey
—The Navy.

In the present chapter, I shall give a brief account of what I saw of the army, that is to say,
of the Nizam Jedeed, (troops disciplined according to the European system,) and, avoid
ing details, shall merely touch upon its general
features.

I had many opportunities of seeing the
greater part of the different corps of cavalry,
infantry, and artillery, both under arms and

in their barracks; and certainly every facility
was kindly offered me. Among other instances,
I was permitted to enter the seraglio, where
some of the cavalry of the Guard were quartered; they were drilled twice a week by Colonel Calosso, known in the army as Rustam
Bey, whom, on these occasions, I used to ac-
company; I used also, at the same time, to be
provided with a military-equipped charger.

The guard consists of three regiments of
cavalry, and three of infantry. Its corps still
retain the name of Bostanjis. The line comprises
nine regiments of cavalry, and sixteen of infantry. The regiments of cavalry are composed
of six squadrons, each of ninety-six horses,
forming a total of six thousand nine hundred
and twelve horses. Three other regiments were
raising, which, when complete, would increase
the force to eight thousand six hundred and

forty horses. The flank squadrons of each regiment were organized as lancers. The men
are armed with sabres, made according to the
old English light-dragoon model, a carbine
slung from the belt, and not fixed in the
bucket, and a pair of pistols : the lancer squadrons have no carbines. The horses are small,
but active ; they are chiefly taken from Mol-
davia and Bosnia, and have as yet cost the
sultan very little, being mostly presents from
different pashas and wealthy individuals. Very
great attention is not paid to grooming them ;
but the forage issued out is sufficient. The
saddles and bridles are English, and are made
on the Hussar principle ; but, instead of using
a folded blanket as we do, they employ several
layers of felt joined together, which material,
they say, experience has taught them to be best
adapted for preventing sore backs.

I did not observe much uniformity of system

in the manner of riding, nor can this as yet be
expected, considering how much the new mode
differs from the old and national one; besides
which, the sultan was much too anxious to see
his cavalry embodied for work to allow the ne-
cessary time for a regular course of riding les-
sons. The officers, however, and many of the
men, take great pains to acquire the new seat,
and much pride in showing it off when obtained ; the principal objection entertained by the
men, appeared to me to consist of being obliged to wear straps to their overalls; for I observed that most of them, whenever favourable
opportunities presented themselves for doing so
without being seen, leant down and unbuttoned
them, so that in a short time manv naked legs
became visible, the overalls flying up.

The dress of the officers of the Guard, when
in full uniform, consists of blue jackets and
overalls; the former are covered with gold-chain

lace, and exactly resemble the full dress of
our 7th Hussars. In undress, they wear a blue
frock-coat, with red collar and cuffs. The
men are also in blue, with the red facing and
three large red stars, or suns, worked on each
side of the centre row of the buttons, and their
overalls have double red stripes. Both officers
and men wear the simple red fez.

The exercising ground in the seraglio lies
between the deer park and the Theodosian
column. The sultan does not, at present, devote so much of his time to drilling his cavalry
as formerly; his leisure hours being chiefly
taken up with literary pursuits, especially the
study of Arabic poetry ; he himself is said to
write with considerable grace ; and the Hatti
Shereefs, which are generally remarkable for
force and elegance, are of his own composition.

Rustam Bey put the troops, for two hours a day, through a great variety of manœuvres, some of which were very complicated; they were all performed on the move and not from the halt, and generally at a canter, or accelerated trot. I was quite astonished to find with what general precision they were all executed; in the charges, however, owing to the great variety and quality of the horses, there was not quite the *ensemble* that might be desired; but the pace was good. It was, on these occasions, rather nervous for the spectators, who were ranged with their horses' croup close to the wall; for the halt was never made till the mizraklus (lancers) touched the said wall with the point of their lances. I often could not help dreading that some of these spear-heads might be made to go through my body instead of being directed to the right or left

of it. Some wild, lively boy, disposed to gra-
tify his desire of sticking an infidel, might afterwards have excused himself by saying, that
the dust prevented his seeing ; however, I never
felt more than the flags wiping the dust off my
moustaches.

Their code of manœuvres is copied from the
one introduced about eighteen months ago in
France.   On the whole, their state of discipline, and their manner of working, reflect the
highest credit on Colonel Calosso, especially
when the numerous and violent prejudices he
had, on commencing, to contend against, and
his ignorance at first of the Turkish language,
are fairly considered.   He now speaks the language fluently, and, what is more important, is
a great favourite with both officers and men.

Some of the regiments, during the late war,
greatly distinguished themselves, and, on se-

veral occasions, completely annihilated whole
corps of Russians, cavalry as well as infantry.
On one occasion, one of the cavalry regiments,
commanded by a colonel with whom I was
acquainted, (but who was not the person who
related the affair to me,) was marching along
a raised causeway of great length, when it
came upon three Russian battalions,—it immediately charged, cut the first to pieces, broke
through the second, and drove the third before
it. This is no contemptible *fait d'armes* for
any cavalry.

The cavalry barracks in the seraglio are
just behind the Balyk kioshk, and form a hollow square; one room runs round the whole,
which allows a free circulation of air ; down the
centre is a row of wooden pillars supporting a
beam and shelf, on which are placed and suspended the kit and arms ; four rows of inclined

planes like our guard-room beds, and raised
about nine inches from the floor, run round
both sides; and in double rows down the
middle of them, are the mats which compose
the soldiers' beds.

In the officers' mess-room, I used to smoke
and drink caravan tea, which, in many instances, has taken the place of coffee. I also
used to frequent the odas of the pages, situated
in the great palace of the seraglio. Most,
if not all the officers, are taken from the corps
of these pages.

Regimental tailors, boot-makers, &c., had
just been established.

The pay of the officers and men is, for the
country, liberal; for example, a colonel receives
one thousand two hundred piastres (£16.) a
month; besides which he is furnished, at the
expense of government, with horses, uniform,

appointments, rations, — in fact, with every thing.

The infantry consists of three regiments of the guard, and sixteen of the line, each of which is composed of five taburs or battalions, four of which are for service; the others form the depôt. A battalion has eight companies or ortaluks, of one hundred men each; the company is divided into twelve behluks, sub-divisions or pelotons; the eighth ortaluk of each battalion is organized as *voltigeurs*; and the fourth battalion of each regiment is drilled to act as sharpshooters or skirmishers. The war-strength of each company is one hundred and seventy men. This gives, therefore, ex-clusive of officers, non-commissioned officers and the depôts, an effective force in peace of sixty thousand eight hundred bayonets.

Each regiment is commanded by a miralai;

a battalion by a bim bashi; and a company by
a yuz bashi, having under him two melazems
or lieutenants. Each battalion has a sagh
aghasi and a sol aghasi, ranks which the French
call *adjudants de la droite et de la gauche*. The
names of the inferior ranks are bairakdar, or
standard-bearer; chaoosh bashi, sergeant major;
chaoosh, sergeant; ou bashi, corporal; trom-
petji bashi, drum major; chialghiji bashi, band
master; baltaji bashi, sergeant of pioneers.
One of the regiments forms a corps of marines,
called Terskhaneh taboor. Eight regiments
are quartered in Constantinople or its immediate vicinity.

The men are steady under arms, manœuvre
with tolerable precision, and their lines and
coverings are correct: their arms are kept clean
and in good order, and the barrels of their
muskets burnished. In their dress and appoint-

ments, however, they look dirty and slovenly; and, wearing no stock round the neck, have an undress appearance. The privates are all very young men, and many are mere boys of twelve years old, who can hardly carry their firelocks; but it is not for want of grown-up men that we find these boys in the ranks,—it is purposely done, and on a sound principle; for these boys never having possessed any of the power and consequence of the Janizaries, and never having known any other system of discipline and instruction than the now existing one, will form, in a few years, a fine steady army, on which the sultan may rely with confidence, which could not be the case if its component parts consisted wholly, or in part, of the turbulent spirits of the old school.

The military bands perform very well, and are under the instruction of Donizetti, brother of the famous Neapolitan composer. The young Turks show a great disposition for music.

The barracks are fine spacious buildings, placed in airy and healthy situations.

The pay in the line is five hundred piastres a month for a bim bashi; three hundred for a yuz bashi; and one hundred and fifty for a melazem.

I several times witnessed their artillery practice, which was tolerable. The topjis, (artillery-men,) the khumbarajis, (bombardiers,) the baltajis, (sappers,) and the laghumjis, (miners,) are divided into regiments. Each battery is composed of four field-pieces and two howitzers. Four batteries form a regiment of twenty-four *bouches à feu*, and as many *caissons*. The old pieces of one and a half, three, and five pounders, have been replaced by new ones of seven, nine, and eleven.

The division quartered at Dolma-baghcheh, used to assemble twice a week on the downs by the road to Therapia, not far from the Yldiz kioshk, when the sultan himself used to attend, and on several occasions pointed the guns, and was far from making the worst shots.

The commander of the artillery is Tahir Pasha, who commanded the Turkish fleet at Navarin. He was shortly going to Varna to re-establish the fortifications of that place. The second in command is Kara Jehennem, or Black-Hell. He is the officer who distinguished himself so much in quieting the Janizaries in the Et Meidan, and who also behaved with so much gallantry against the Russians near Shumla.

Promotion in the army is given for merit, and not by interest or seniority, as the following extract from one of their military gazettes

will show :—" Muhammed Bey, colonel of the
1st regiment of the 1st brigade, and his lieutenant-colonel, Hassan Bey, having shown but
little capacity and zeal in the military service,
and in the execution of the functions attached
to their respective ranks, have been dismissed.
An examination having been held among the
officers next in rank for the purpose of re-
placing them, Aly Bey, lieutenant-colonel
of the 2nd regiment of the 2nd brigade, and
Kavakli Emin Bey, major in the 2nd regiment of the 1st brigade, having shown the
greatest knowledge in the theory of war, and
in the details of discipline, have been promoted to the vacancies. Their places also, after
a strict examination, have been filled up by
Asmi Efendi, commanding the 2nd battalion
of the 2nd regiment of the 2nd brigade, and
by Eumer Bey, major in the same corps. This

latter officer has been succeeded by Mustafa, son of Yusuf, Pasha of Seres."

This is a proper system, and worthy of being imitated.

There are six large hospitals for the troops and navy; three for the army in general—namely, those at Top-kapoo, Mal-depeh, and Top Tash; one for the artillery, another for the *ouvriers militaires*, and one for the navy. Independent of these, each regiment and each ship has its own private hospital.

Should another war break out in the course of a few years between the Othmanlus and Russians, when the Turkish army and navy are complete in their organization and discipline, the result, I feel convinced, will be far different from that of the last; and no more marshals or generals will then have grounds on which to found claims to the title of Sabal-

kanski.   Although, during the late campaigns,
the Turks were vanquished after the greatest
efforts on the part of Russia, yet, in the
struggle, Russia lost no less than one hundred
and eighty thousand men, and a great part of
her artillery; the *prestige* of the Russian arms,
so much spoken of and so much dreaded in
Europe, was completely destroyed; and the
world saw, to its utter astonishment, that the
Moslems, though labouring under the greatest
possible disadvantages, were able to subdue,
with a weak and undisciplined force, more than
double their own number of their foe's best
troops.

In 1827-28, the Russian force amounted to
eight hundred and sixty-four thousand five
hundred men; namely, one hundred and sixty-
nine thousand four hundred cavalry, four hundred and one thousand infantry, forty-seven

thousand artillery, twenty-seven thousand of
extra corps, two hundred thousand extraordinary levies, and twenty thousand officers. By
far the greater portion of these forces were composed of old and well-disciplined soldiers, commanded by experienced officers, provided with
every possible thing requisite to carry on war-
fare, and, from the uniform system of their organization and instruction, acting with that perfect *ensemble* so conducive to success. Russia
was tranquil at home, had no other foreign foe
to oppose, and the emperor was a favourite with
his subjects. On the other hand, the Othmanlus, during the war, never had, at any one time,
more than eighty thousand men under arms.
The brave and determined Janizaries, the da-
ring and impetuous Delhis and Spahis, and the
active and harassing Timariots of the days of
Selim and Suleyman, no longer existed ; in their

places, were from twenty to thirty thousand raw,
weak, and inexperienced boys, to whom, at that
period, it would have been thought a burlesque
to have applied the term of "regular troops;"
the rest of the army was made up of wild and
lawless Asiatics.   No money, no depôts, no ma-
gazines, no commissariat, and, worse than all, no
experienced officers.   Turkey had just been agitated by a great and dreadful revolution ; and,
in the very midst of the war, another serious
insurrection broke out.   The Sultan was de-
tested by a powerful faction for the innovations
he had introduced.   This disaffection was, by
Russian gold, converted into open treason:
Varna was basely surrendered, the Balkan was
left undefended, and the Pasha of Iskondrah,
with a considerable army, preserved a shame-
ful state of inactivity,—and yet, what were the
results of the first campaign ?   Why, the Rus-

sians, after having suffered immense losses, and their army being perfectly disorganized and demoralized, were obliged with the greatest haste to retire behind the Danube, leaving behind them the greater part of their *matériel.*

During the second campaign it is true that, assisted by the treachery of some pashas, they did succeed in reaching Adrianople; but, arrived there, they found they had only eighteen thousand men wherewith to follow up their operations. The Turks had forty thousand men in their rear at Sofia; but these were, by the traitor who commanded them, not suffered to act; though, *after* the signature of the peace, he blustered and threatened much, thereby hoping to conceal his infamy. There is also no doubt that the Russians, aware of their own weakness, and of the unpleasant predicament in which they found themselves, were far more anxious for peace than the Sultan, who only required to be properly supported by his subjects to have come out of the contest as a conqueror. Fortunate would it have proved for him, if his enemies had advanced against the capital, for then the whole population, throwing off their apathy, and recollecting that the seat of their empire and religion was in danger, would have risen *en masse*, and the consequence would probably have been, that not one single man of the " accursed yellow-haired giaours" would have returned to his own dreary *steppes*. But unfortunately the Turks, not aware of the miserable plight of the invaders of their country, signed the humiliating treaty — and the world praised the barbaric northern tyrant for his magnanimity in sparing a prostrate enemy, at the time when he himself, in private, was singing a *Te Deum* for his fortunate escape from annihilation.

Little as I have said of the army, I can say still less of the navy, not being very conversant with maritime affairs.

At Terskhaneh, I saw all that part of the Turkish navy which was then in the harbour of the capital. With the exception of two frigates, one of which was the Raphael, captured from the Russians in the Black Sea during the late war, and three corvettes, kept in commission as schools of instruction for young officers and naval recruits : all the rest were in ordinary, and consisted of

9 Ships of the line,
2 Double-banked frigates,
9 Frigates,
14 Corvettes,
2 Brigs,

1 Cutter,

2 Steam vessels.

I could not ascertain the number of ships in commission or laid up in other ports, but the following is a list of those on the stocks in different dock-yards :—

No.	Guns.	Length in feet.	Where building.
1	84	137	Sinope.
1	80	135	Ghemlek.
1	80	134	Boudroom.
1	60	130½	Erkli.
1	48	114½	Rhodes.
1	48	113½	Ghidros.
1	46	118½	Fazza.
1	46	106	Samson.
1	46	106	Amasreh.
1	46	106	Bartin.
1	50	111	Lemnos.
1	46	106	Akcheh Shehr.
1	46	106	Ismid.
1	48	106	Mytelene.

Besides which, there were several corvettes, brigs, schooners, and smaller vessels.

We visited the Mahmoodieh, a three-decker, measuring in extreme length, two hundred and fifty-six feet, and pierced for one hundred and thirty-two guns, six of which were brass three-hundred pounders. She had only lately been launched, and the workmen were still employed in fitting up the cabin, which was to be inlaid with a great variety of beautiful woods, the growth of Turkey. On board, we became acquainted with Hassan Bey, the Capudana Bey,* said to be the best sailor in the navy.

Halil Pasha is the Capudan Pasha. This man, not many years ago, was a slave at the Dardanelles; but, having obtained his freedom, and being pushed on by his former master,

* There are several officers called Sanjak-beys, whose rank answers to that of rear-admirals.

the serasker, his fortunes rose rapidly. At the conclusion of the last war with Russia, he was sent as ambassador to Petersburgh: he is now commander-in-chief of the navy, and is shortly to be married to one of the Sultan's daughters.

Alongside of the Mahmoodieh was the Selim, an old three-decker, not much inferior in size, and possessing the invaluable qualification of being a good sailer under all circumstances, whether well navigated and trimmed, or the reverse, on or off a wind, in a gale, or in a calm.

With the exception, I believe, of the Pennsylvania American line-of-battle ship, the Mahmoodieh is the largest in the world. The Pasha of Egypt is also building some very large ships; one of which, the Mehalet el Kebeer, measures, along her water-line, two hundred and twelve feet, is fifty-eight feet in

the beam, and is to fight one hundred and
thirty-six guns. Timber is very cheap in
Turkey, selling for one English penny the
cubic foot; and, some years back, the expense
of building a first-rate in the Black Sea amounted only to about 9,000*l*. One of the double-
banked frigates had just come round from the
Black Sea, where she had been launched. She
was a very fine vessel, but looked, alongside
of the Mahmoodieh, like a small boat. Another of the frigates had also arrived from Si-
zeboli, where she had been sunk during the
war, but subsequently got up. The cutter
had lately been launched, and was built on the
exact model of the English cutter Hind.

None of the ships are ever painted till they
have been rigged.

The largest of the steam vessels, formerly one
of the English packets to Hamburgh, was com-

manded by Captain Kelly, an Englishman who
has entered the Turkish service. He was excessively civil to us, taking us over all the different departments of the arsenal, and on board
the men-of-war. This steam vessel is fitted up
as a yacht for the Sultan, who frequently makes
excursions in her.

The ships in commission seemed very neatly
rigged, and were particularly light and clear
aloft. I was especially struck with the Shereef
Rezan, a beautiful new frigate.

Captain Kelly, (who speaks Turkish remarkably well, and is a great favourite with the
Capudan Pasha and his brother officers,) took
us also over the dock-yard, where we visited
the store-houses, forges, rope-walks, mast-sheds,
&c. A great part of the workmen consisted of
Albanians, lately taken prisoners by the vizir
during the insurrection of their country. We

also inspected two very fine dry docks for repairing the larger ships, one built by Selim III., the other by the present Sultan. Under one of the sheds, in which the Sultan's state barges are kept, we were shown one which belonged to Muhammed II., the conqueror of Constantinople.

The following is a curious instance either of carelessness or of a strong belief in predestination on the part of the Turks. Halil, the present Capudan Pasha, on first coming to office, was looking out for some building in which to establish a forge and an armourer's shop. One was pointed out to him as adapted for the purpose, which, on being opened, was found, much to his surprise, to be quite full of loaded shells and grenades with the fuzes in them, and a great quantity of loose powder scattered about in all directions; this building, (which by-the-bye, I think must originally have been a chapel during the Western Empire,) had several open windows. Some considerable fires had lately committed great ravages in its immediate vicinity, yet *every day* fires were lighted against its walls, either for the pitch cauldrons, or for cooking the men's messes, and this system continued for many years without the occurrence of a single accident. How great is Providence!

We also visited the Kourek-Zindani, bagno or prison, which is within the enclosure of the Terskhaneh, and is familiar to the recollection of all who have read that delightful book, the Memoirs of Anastasius. It was quite full of occupants, some of whom were of considerable rank. The prisoners are employed in the different works of the arsenal

The prison bazaar is a most dismal-looking

place : it consists of a narrow passage of pitchy darkness, bordered on each side with small, miserable shops, each having, in its farthest recess, one wretched, gloomy lamp, struggling in vain to give light on this scene of misery, but barely sufficient, in fact, to make the darkness visible.

At the end of this passage, having first passed, in almost total darkness, the crowds of savage, ferocious, and desperate-looking personages, the rattling of whose chains told us that murder or robbery had ushered them into this den, there is a chapel of the Greeks. On first entering it, we found ourselves in the most perfect obscurity; but, on paying a few paras, the candles were lighted. Its altars and walls were decorated with images, pictures, and other ornaments ; the pictures represented the Virgin and a variety of saints, and were of very ancient and curious execution : the back-ground of the

pictures was in gold leaf, and the dresses of
the saints in solid silver. Among these different
portraits was one of St. Nicholas, taken from
the captured Russian frigate, the Raphael.

When the Turks took possession of this
vessel, they found the image over an altar,
surrounded with a great number of wax candles
and lamps; these they immediately lighted,
and, seating themselves round it, commenced
smoking their chibooks. It must have formed
a curious little picture — this little *réunion*
of Mussulmeen, with eyes fixed on the portrait
of the worthy St. Nicholas, surrounded by his
staff of candles, relics, artificial flowers, &c.,
offering up to him clouds of the fragrant smoke
of Saloniki and Latakia, perhaps just as agreeable to him as that of frankincense.

CHAPTER XI.

Walls and Gates of Constantinople—Abattoirs—Church
of the Fish—Siege of Constantinople by Muhammed
—The Seven Towers—Visit to the Efendi's Harem—
The Eski Serai—Tekkehs of the Derwishes—Burial-
ground at Scutari.

PERHAPS the most interesting walk about Constantinople, is that leading round the city, outside the walls on the land side, extending from
the Yedi Koulleler to the Haivan Serai, (palace
of the wild beasts.)

The best mode of visiting the walls, is to
take a kaeek, either at Topkhaneh or Galata, and
to pull close to the Seraglio Point, from which
you gently glide down the stream, keeping
close in shore, which is bordered by the walls of

the seraglio; behind rise lofty cypresses, and
the different masses and towers of the imperial palaces, together with the Theodosian
column. Two or three little doors are seen,
cut through the walls; through these many a
fair but frail Odalek has passed, on her way to
her watery grave.

At the end of the seraglio wall, are two little
kioshks built over the water;—the one used
as the place of trial for vizirs, the other as
the place of their execution. Just behind it,
and within the walls, are the cavalry barracks
of the guard.

Hence we proceed along the old and unre-
paired walls of the town, passing by the following gates, Chatladi-kapoo, Koom-kapoo, Yeni-
kapoo, Daood Pasha-kapoo, Psamatia-kapoo,
and Narli-kapoo. In parts, the walls are entirely destroyed, but by far the greater por-

tion, together with the square towers, still exist in very tolerable preservation. Imbedded in them are a variety of fragments of columns, cornices, inscriptions, &c.

Landing at the angle formed by the wall turning inland from the sea, you find yourself close to the famous fortress of Yedi Koulleler, which I shall hereafter describe; and, close to the water on the left hand, is a large wooden building, called the Sal-khaneh, where all the cattle and sheep destined for the use of the capital are slaughtered : it is, in fact, a similar establishment to the *abattoirs* of Paris.

Proceeding onwards, the upper part of the Golden Gate is seen rising above the walls. The first entrance into the city, called Yedi Koulleler-kapoo, is close to it.

A little before arriving at the next gate, (the Selivri-kapoo,) through which passes the

road to Silivria, are seen on the left, close to
the road side, the tombs of Aly, Pasha of
Yanina, and of four members of his family—
namely, his three sons, Veli, Muhktar, and
Saalih, and his grandson, Muhammed the son
of Veli ; the first of these was a pasha of three
tails, the others of two. Muhktar is the hero
commemorated in the following lines by Lord
Byron.

" Dark Muchtar his son to the Danube is sped,
Let the yellow-haired Giaours view his horse-tails
 with dread ;
When his Delhis come dashing in blood o'er the
 banks,
How few shall escape from the Muscovite ranks !"

Rebellion caused the fall of this powerful
and talented family: their heads alone were
buried here by one of their friends, after hav-

ing been exposed to the public gaze in the court of the seraglio.

From these tombs, a road turning to the left leads to the ruins of Balukli kalissa, " the church of the fish." We descended to what were formerly the under-ground vaults of the edifice, (though now they are open to the sky,) and observed, in a stream of water, some small flat fish swimming about, and also a number of bright new paras at the bottom, the votive offerings of the pious. The story related to us on the spot respecting these fish, condensed in a few words, was as follows:—

During the siege of Constantinople by Muhammed II., the news being brought to this church that the Othmanlus had actually penetrated into the city, the monk, whose duty it was to cook for the rest, and who was at that moment frying some fish, firm in the belief that

the city was under the special protection of
his saints, boldly asserted that the story was
false, adding, that it was as probable that the
fish he was then frying should return to life,
as that the city should be taken by the infidels.
Scarce had these words escaped from his lips,
when behold !—the fish did actually jump out
of the frying pan, not into the fire, but into
the little stream flowing close by, and commenced swimming about, and amusing themselves as gaily as if their skins had never been
under the destructive influence of boiling oil;
and these fish we were now looking at were
the identical individuals to whom the miracle
had happened. We showed our belief of the
story by presenting them with our quota of
paras, and so departed.

After passing Yeni-kapoo, we came to the
Top-kapoo, or Cannon Gate, so called from

four large shot being fixed in the wall above
it. Through this the victor Muhammed made
his triumphal entry. On the undulating ground
opposite to it, and near the military hospital,
is a mound called Mal-depeh, on whose summit, during the siege, proudly waved the
Turkish standard, and from which the haughty
Sultan beheld with exultation the last bulwarks
of the Greek empire crumbling beneath the
resistless assaults of his gallant warriors. Between this gate and the Edrene-kapoo, or
Adrianople Gate, the ground sinks into a little
valley, through which, at times, flows a small
stream, which, after passing through the Yeni-
baghcheh and the rest of the city, falls into
the sea at the Armenian quarter between Daood
Pasha-kapoo and Yeni-kapoo.

On the slope of this valley, is still seen the
breach made by the Turks, who themselves

thus describe it :—" The gates and ramparts
of Constantinople soon became like the heart of
an unfortunate lover—they were pierced in a
thousand places." It was on this breach that
Constantine, the last of the Paleologi, is supposed to have met his death, whilst gallantly
defending the last remnant of his empire ; there
is, however, every reason to regard the story,
in its generally-received form, as the offspring
of vanity on the part of the Greeks and
Christians generally, who wished to throw a
gleam of light and glory on the last of their
weak and effeminate sovereigns. Saed-ed-Deen,
who has always been considered an impartial
and faithful historian, thus relates the circum-
stance in his Taj Al Towareekh, or " Diadem
of History :"—" The Othmanlus, regarding
their lives as common merchandise, mounted
to the assault with intrepidity, by the breaches

which had been made on the south side of the
Adrianople Gate. They penetrated beyond
the ramparts, when the advanced-guard of
darkness appeared in the western horizon. On
this, Sultan Muhammed ordered his soldiers
to fix lanterns and lights on the points of their
spears and lances, in order to prevent the Christians from repairing the breaches. According
to this imperial mandate, the light of the
torches and lamps illumined the front of the
city and the environs, which became like a
plain covered with roses and tulips. On the
following morning, the general of the Franks
mounted on the ramparts in order to repel the
Mussulmeen. At this moment, a young Moslem,* taking the cord of firm resolution, threw

* To most readers, it is unnecessary to mention
that "Moslem" is the singular, "Mussulmeen" the
plural.

himself like a spider upon the walls, and having vigorously employed his crescent-moon-
shaped sabre, at one blow sent forth the soul
of the infidel from his body, like an owl
from its impure nest. The Mussulmeen then
crowded towards the breaches, assured that
they were the gates of victory, and soon raised
their triumphant beyraks and sanjaks on the
walls.* The Greek emperor, who, together
with his *élite*, was in his palace on the north of
the Adrianople Gate, having learnt that some
of the Othmanlus had already entered, fled,
and on his way discovered some of the victors
who, full of confidence, had commenced pil-
laging. At this, the fire of hate filled his dark

* The attacking columns opposite Top-kapoo were
commanded by Nishani, *alias* Karamani Muhammed
Pasha. Those opposite Edrene-kapoo, by Saadi
Pasha.

soul, and, rushing upon these unsuspecting Mussulmeen, his scythe-like sabre gathered the harvest of their lives. One poor soldier of this band, who was only wounded, bathed in the blood which flowed from his wounds, and full of anguish, awaited the approach of death. The Greek king, beholding this wretch, raised his sword to take his last breath. In this moment of despair, the unhappy soldier, aided by Divine assistance, dragged this enemy of the faith from his gold-adorned saddle, and cast him on the dark earth, making his warlike scimitar descend upon his head."

This probably is the plain unvarnished statement of the affair. The very fact of Constantine being on horseback, proves that he could not well have been upon the summit of the breach — at least, I believe it is not custo-

mary to place cavalry on the ramparts of a
town.*

Within the walls, and near the Edrene-
kapoo, is a mosque, built by the lovely Mihrumah, the daughter of Suleyman I.   Between
this gate and the next one, called, from its form,
Egri-kapoo, (the crooked gate,) is a large
old building, called Tekir Serai, supposed
by some to be the Hebdomon, one of Constantine's palaces, by others, the habitation of Beli-
sarius.   Over one of the windows is the following escutcheon.

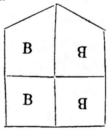

* The body of Constantine is said to have been
buried in the Sulu Menasteer, or water monastery.

It is, at all events, the palace alluded to in the above extract from Saed-ed-Deen, as the one where the last Constantine was, at the time of the Turks' entrance into the city.

Descending the hill, you again enter the town at the Haivan Serai, and taking a kaeek at the first stairs, are soon conveyed to Galata.

This walk, as I before observed, is excessively beautiful and highly interesting, whilst the still silence and solitude which reign over the scene, though so close to the large and busy capital of the eastern world, is very striking. The walls themselves, especially between Egri-kapoo and Haivan Serai, are remarkably picturesque, being covered in many places with ivy, creepers, and shrubs, whilst, in the space between the different walls, grow many trees. They have suffered much from earthquakes, and some of the large towers are actually rent

I 2

from the summit to their base, whilst the por
tions inclining outwards, seem to threaten in-
stant destruction to the passers-by.

The walls are triple, having a ditch twenty-
five feet wide in front ; the first and lowest
rises about twelve or fourteen feet above the
present bottom of the ditch, and has only a
parapet. Twenty-five feet in rear of this, is
the second, fortified with circular towers; and,
at the same distance behind it, rises the third
and highest, strengthened by large square
towers, which divide the intervals between the
round ones of the second line. The walls and
towers are all crenated. In numerous parts,
are inscriptions encased in the walls.

The view from Tekir Serai is extremely
beautiful, embracing the harbour or the Golden
Horn, the Valley of the sweet waters, Kalidzi
Oglou, the extensive barracks of the topjis,

the cannon-foundery, Sudlujy, Eyoob and its
mosque, where the Sultans are crowned, or rather, where they are girded with the sword of
power, and the two palaces, Ramas Chiftlek and
Otakji-keui; whilst, on the right, are the venerable walls of Istambool, which here rise to a
much greater height than in any other part,
and are defended by variously shaped towers,
some of them octagonal. A number of fine
old cypresses and large plane trees, shading
several cafés, complete the picture.

Our ambassador having obtained from the
Porte a firman to visit the Seven Towers, we
proceeded there with him in his state kaeek,
accompanied also by Mr. d'Israeli, Mr. Clay,
and Mr. Meredith. Landing at Narli-kapoo,
we walked to the fortress, where we were
received by the governor, Ibrahim Efendi.
Having conducted us all over it, he gave us

pipes, coffee, pomegranates, and other fruits, in the room formerly set apart for captive foreign ambassadors. It was a light and comfortable room, not bearing the least appearance of a prison.

Lady Temple, whilst we proceeded to enjoy our pipes, went to pay a visit to the Efendi's wives in the harem. She found only three; two of whom were old and plain, but the third was young and pretty. A continued exchange of words was carried on between the two parties, though the one understood not a word of any Christian language, and the other was as little versed in that of Turkey; there was no terjemaness to explain the civil speeches which were said on both sides, yet they parted as great friends as if they had understood them all.

The fortress of the Seven Towers was erected by Muhammed II., on the site of the ancient

fort, called by the Greeks, from its form, Cy-
clobion. Although it still retains the name of
Yedi-koulleler, yet only four of the towers at
present exist entire, the fortress having suffered
greatly from the earthquake of 1768. On the
walls are mounted a few small and very old
pieces of artillery. In the towers the prisoners
of war were confined, and the names of persons of all nations, some of them connected
with remote dates, are seen carved on the
stones. At present, the castle is used as a
dépôt for gunpowder; within its enclosure,
there is also a mesjid and several other buildings.

Within, or rather forming part of its walls,
and facing the Propontis, is the famous Porta
Aurea, constructed of white marble. It consists of three arches, but these are now all
blocked up, with the exception of a little door

left in the centre one, which opens upon the narrow space between it and the city walls. The centre arch is flanked by two Corinthian pilasters; and in different parts are seen remains of frieze and cornice. On each side of the gate, and connected with it, advances a large, square, and well-preserved tower, on the summit of one of the angles of which, is a well-executed and uninjured eagle with expanded wings. This is, however, all that remains of its former splendour; the different bas-reliefs mentioned by Wheler, which represented the fall of Phaëton, Hercules and Cerberus, Venus and Adonis, &c., have all passed away,* as well as the inscription stating the

* Perhaps a little excavation in the garden, and an inspection of the materials of which the houses are built, would bring some of these pieces of sculpture to light.

gate to have been constructed by Theodosius, in commemoration of his victory over Maximus. It was as follows :—

HAEC LOCA THEODOSIVS DECORAT POST FATA
TYRANNI
AVREA SAECLA GERIT QVI PORTAM CONSTRVIT
AVRO.

The Sultan has a small kioshk overlooking the walls, in which detained diplomatists were occasionally allowed to recreate themselves.

I was very much pleased at having been enabled to visit the interior of this fortress, as but very few persons indeed, prisoners excepted, have ever been allowed admittance, and I had myself several times before, in vain, tried the effect of gold on the dragons who guard it.

The best general and panoramic view of Constantinople and the surrounding country, is obtained from the summit of the Serasker's tower in the court of the Eski Serai, built on the site of the ancient Janizaries' tower by the present Serasker, Hosrew Mehemmed Pasha. It is solidly constructed of stone, with a wooden spiral stair leading to a gallery with windows all round, and one hundred and seventy-one feet above the court-yard. The total height to the gilt crescent on the summit, is two hundred and twenty feet.

The Eski Serai, which was built in 1454 by Muhammed II. for his harem, on the site of a monastery, is no longer appropriated for its original purpose, but forms the residence of the commander-in-chief, and within its precincts are the different offices connected with the department of war. Here are also the

quarters of the Chaooshes, Ghawasses, Yasakjis, and Tatars, who compose the body-guard of
the Serasker, and who are to be daily seen assembled in groups, at the great gate fronting the mosque of Sultan Bayazeed, and presenting, from the variety and brilliant colours
of their gold-embroidered costumes, and the
glitter of their costly arms, the appearance of
a gaudy bed of tulips.

At Galata is another lofty tower, from which
also was formerly obtained a very extensive
view; but the staircase which led to the summit, and the conical roof, were lately destroyed
by fire.

These towers were erected in order that vi-
dettes stationed there might be able to give
an early alarm in case of fire, and, by signals,
point out the quarter in which it had broken
out. In the circular room, from whose win-

dows you look out upon the surrounding scenery, a *café* is established, and many derwishes meet there to read the Koran.

A propos of these worthies, a visit to their tekkehs should not be omitted, at least to two of them, the Spinners at Pera, and the Howlers at Scutari.

The former, who are of the sect of Mevlevi, perform every Friday at two o'clock; their tekkeh is in the main street of Pera, and close to the *Petit champ des Morts*. The first time we went there, we were rather early, and waited some time in the yard, which was filled with crowds of all descriptions and ranks, including a considerable number of soldiers. The doors were at last opened, and we entered; but the sentries made us take off our boots and shoes. The interior of the building is octagonal, with a lower and upper gallery run-

ning round it; there were also some rooms
above partitioned off by gratings, and reserved
for the Turkish ladies. The area was formed
of highly polished wood, like the *parquets* of
Paris.

Eight derwishes soon after came into the
arena, and seated themselves, crossed-legged,
round it. The chief had a green shawl twisted
round the base of his lofty conical cap. Prayers
were then both read and sung, accompanied by
strange wild music. After some time, the derwishes threw off their cloaks and walked so-
lemnly round the area, having their arms folded
over their breasts. Whenever they passed by
a red carpet at the head of the room, where
the chief had been seated, they made low pros-
trations before it. After several turns, they commenced waltzing till each had occupied a place
where he might spin on his own ground with-

out interfering with the evolutions of his comrades; their feet were naked, and their hands
held up, on one of which they kept their eyes
fixed, I imagine to prevent giddiness; they wore
tight waistcoats, with long and very ample petti-
coats, which, in their revolutions, spread themselves out into immense circles.   The chief did
not spin.   Music played the whole time of the
performance, which was divided into three acts.
At the conclusion of the last, we all broke up,
feeling, I believe, much more giddy than the
actors.   During the spectacle, I was much astonished at being thus addressed, in very
good English, by an individual seated next to
me:—" Well, sir, what do you think of all
this d—d nonsense ?"   I soon discovered that
he was an Egyptian whom I had slightly
known at Kahira, and who had been sent by
the Pasha of England there to obtain an European education.

The tekkeh of the howling derwishes, of the
sect of Rufăhí, is at Iskiudar, or Scutari, at
the edge of the town.

The room was small and dirty, and the walls
covered with pictures, if Arabic sentences,
twisted into the representation of different
figures, may be so called. In the open space in
the centre, was stationed a rank of performers,
who were incessantly employed in bending
their bodies from the hips upwards, back-
ward and forward, throwing, at the same time,
their weight alternately from leg to leg, and
singing forth, in varied cadences, the name of
Allah, the sounds seeming to proceed from the
bottom of the stomach. Two or three derwishes assisted them to keep time by singing
and beating their tamborines and cymbals.
This ceremony lasted so long, and the exertion
was so great, that one or two of the actors

dropped down from complete exhaustion. This
affair concluded by a second act, in which the
derwishes struck daggers through the faces
and into the breasts of their disciples, leaving
the weapons,(to the handles of which were fixed,
by chains, six-pound cannon-balls,) sticking
in the wounds: many of the persons performed
this part of the ceremony with their own hands.
After they had remained for several minutes,
the chief derwish advanced and drew them out,
touching the wounds and appearing instantly
to heal them. The whole scene was very
curious, and certainly proved these jugglers to
belong to the first class of their profession ; for
they performed these acts with so much cool-
ness and quiet, and gave you so much time
to watch all their movements, that it was difficult to persuade oneself that they had not in
reality performed a miracle.

I have already observed, that the great and
well-known burial ground of Scutari com-
mences close to this tekkeh: let nothing prevent the traveller from visiting it—and *alone*.
There is an indescribable sombre beauty in
almost all the Turkish mezarleks, which deeply
and forcibly affects the feelings ; but in this it is
felt a hundred-fold ;—its immense extent,—its
remote antiquity,—the great size of its splendid
cypress trees,—the ashes of the great, whose
names are still alive in the records of fame,—
and the awful silence and deep shadows which
reign over the scene, make an impression which
no lapse of years can ever efface.

The high roads through Analdoly pass through
it, to the west, the east, and the south, and
are of course much frequented ; yet I have in-
variably observed that the scene produces on
all a most marked effect.   Few words are

heard. The lawless and blood-drinking Spahi
of Asia,—the unprincipled and plundering
Moghrabeen,—the wild and reckless Arab,—as
they approach it, are all seen checking uncon-
sciously the pace of their horses; the conversa-
tion gradually decreases, and finally stops; the
pipe is never out of the mouth, the features
relax, and the eye, losing its fire, wanders to the
right and left in quiet contemplation. It is,
however, when at a distance from the road,
and in the depths of the great forest, that these
impressions are most powerfully felt.

How different are the mezarleks of the Othmanlus to our own frightful churchyards, un-
adorned by a single tree, if we occasionally except some hideous and deformed yew, and
resembling a stone-mason's yard overgrown
with nettles. The French have, perhaps, gone
too far the other way; their beautiful ceme-

tery of *Père la Chaise* resembles too much a
pretty and well-kept flower-garden.   The Othmanlus have adopted the proper medium : their
tombs are pretty and even gay, being adorned
with gold inscriptions, on a ground either of
black, white, vermillion, or azure; but the
vivid brilliancy of the colours is subdued by
the shade of the numerous and stately cypresses
which rise high above them, and produce that
soft and quiet half-light which so perfectly
harmonises with the deep and profound silence
which reigns over this vast city of death.

The rank and the sex of the dead are distinguished at a single glance, by the shape of
the stone, and by the turban which crowns
the summit: the latter is not found on the
tombs of females.   Since the abolition of the
Janizaries, the Sultan issued an order that the
tombs of all soldiers and *employés* of govern-

ment should not be surmounted by the turban,
but simply by the red fez; this order, however,
has not always been obeyed, as appears from
what I one day witnessed in the great Turkish
burial-ground of Pera. The Sultan, accompanied by his staff, was on horseback, and there
were also a number of men on foot, with large
axes and hammers, whilst others were busily
occupied in reading the sepulchral inscriptions,
and from time to time made signals to those
with the axes—when immediately a blow was
given, and down rolled a marble turban: they
were those that had been erected, since the or-
donnance, over the bodies of Janizaries. I saw
about a hundred and fifty treated in this manner; they were then collected, and thrown in a
heap close to the guard-room at Fundukli,
where they may probably still be seen.

It would be uninteresting to mention all the

great names that are met with; but there are
two monuments which are certainly curious;
the one a dome, supported by four columns, but
having no inscription, which covers the bones
of the favourite charger of Mahmood I.; the
other points out the spot where a horse of Othman II. lies buried.

In the little burial-ground of Pera, and not
far from the tekkeh of the derwishes, is the
tomb of Count Bonneval, who embraced Islamism, and was known as Ahmed Pasha; he
was commander of Khumbarajis, and died in
1160 of the Hejra.

CHAPTER XII.

Departure of the Mekkah Caravan—Iskiudar and its
environs— Printing Office at Iskiudar — Leander's
Tower—Remains of Justinian's Villa—Daood Pasha
—The Sultan's Greyhounds—Tomb of Barbarossa
—Curious monogram.

On the 28th of December, we went to see the
departure of the great Mekkah caravan from
the seraglio. For this purpose we hired a
shop in the little square near the Yeni-jamaa,
and, preceded by two ghawasses, made our way
through a very dense crowd, chiefly composed
of women, who had already assembled to witness the procession, and took our places. The

gay and various costumes of the men contrasted
well with the uniform whiteness of the yashmaks. Several Turkish ladies of distinction
were drawn up in their arabas and carriages,
among whom I remarked the Sultan's sister.
An open passage in the centre of the street
was preserved by patroles, of regular and irregular troops, and by the Serasker's body-
guard.

The procession having left the seraglio,
where prayers had been offered and blessings
given, now made its appearance. It was headed
by the Sheikh ul-Islam, the Ulemas and Mol-
lahs, all mounted on richly-caparisoned horses;
these were followed by the Sultan's staff in
splendid new uniforms; then came two very
large, fine camels, lineal descendants of the
prophet's own favourite animal; they, however,
do not go to Mekkah, but only as far as Iskiudar, where their place is supplied by others.

who, after having fulfilled their holy duty, are
exempt ever afterwards from all labour ; these
camels bore the Mahmal, containing the Koran
and presents for the sacred shrine.   The Mahmal is covered with richly-embroidered silks,
ostrich features, and a variety of little flags,
and of gold and silver ornaments.   The camels'
heads and necks are also profusely decorated
with shells and beads.   It was curious to observe how proudly conscious these animals
appeared to be of their own consequence, and
of the importance of the ceremony in which
they were engaged.

Now advanced a long train of mules, bearing the pilgrims' baggage ; these animals were
also fantastically and gaily decorated.   The procession was closed by the tent-pitchers, lantern-
bearers, and Arab musicians.   Having arrived
at the edge of the Golden Horn, they embarked
for Iskiudar, under salutes from all the men-of-

war and batteries : thus concluded the first day's march, which was not to be resumed till the 4th January.

Neshib Efendi, the commander of the caravan, a post considered as of the highest honour, invited Sir Robert Gordon and ourselves to breakfast with him at Scutari, in order to witness the final departure of the Hajj. Accordingly, early in the morning, we proceeded from Top-khaneh and landed at Scutari, where we found a number of horses and a regular Christian's carriage, (the present, probably, in former days, of some European monarch,) waiting for us on the quay. The Turkish coachman, in his national costume and turban, seated on the hammercloth, had rather a curious effect.

Passing through the streets of Iskiudar, we stopped at the house of the Muhrdar, or keeper of the seals, where Neshib Efendi had taken up his abode. In front of the gate, and in the court-yard, we observed various preparations for departure—horses saddled and impatiently pawing the ground,—mules loaded, and kicking in dislike at being so, — tekhterawans, adorned with gold lattices, silken curtains, and luxuriant cushions, waiting to receive the voluptuous forms of beautiful women, — highcapped Tatars,—splendidly-dressed ghawasses and chokadars, with their canes of office,—yasakjis, surrojis, and soldiers, all ready booted and armed,—fierce-looking men giving orders, humble ones obeying them,—quarrels, oaths, blows, and execrations,—all combining to form an animated and interesting picture.

Passing through this yard, and a pretty garden still slightly sprinkled with roses and other flowers, we entered an orangery, and were thence ushered into a small but pretty

kioskh which opened upon it. Here we were
served with pipes, beautifully ornamented with
diamonds and enamel flowers worked in high
relief, with coffee in cups of Persian porcelain,
held in zarfs of pure gold, and, like the pipes,
adorned with diamonds and enamel bouquets.

Neshib Efendi's son now made his appearance to apologize for his father's absence, who
was too much occupied to leave the divan.
Breakfast was then served in the garden. It
consisted of a variety of Turkish dishes, chiefly
composed of fish, *laitage*, (including the delicious
yaourt,) and preserved fruits ; but all, or most of
the dishes were *maigre*, as they supposed that
all Christians were of one sect, and did not eat
meat on certain days. The only beverage was
spring-water ; but when we returned to the
kioshk to resume our chibooks, coffee, and large
goblets of excellent Cognac were handed round,

even to Lady Temple—who, on the pipes and coffee being first brought in, had been the cause of much discussion among the attendants.

Some of them were about to present the pipes to the cavaliers first; this was, however, objected to by one of them, who said they should eat dirt by doing so; for he knew from reading, and the accounts of travellers, that in the Firenk-vilaieti, or country of the Franks, women were considered superior to men, and that, in fact, the latter were nothing more than the slaves of the former. The assertion drew forth smiles of incredulity, and the exclamations of " Impossible !" " Nonsense !" But the man was firm, and it was done as he directed, except as regarded the ambassador; for he found it quite impossible to convince his comrades that a woman could ever, in any country, or under any circumstances, be served before an Elchi-Bey.

We were now summoned to remount our horses, and then started for the great burial-ground, where we took up a position to see the caravan defile by us. First came a detachment of irregular cavalry, acting as *éclaireurs*; then a corps of baltajis with red leather aprons, and ancient battle-axes, inlaid with gold; a battalion of the guards, with their band; Neshib Efendi, and a brilliant staff; a great number of tekhterawans, with the women and children of the principal officers; mules carrying two large square panniers, one on each side, and each containing a woman; the whole being covered by green tents or awnings. The rear was brought up by a number of pilgrims; the greater portion of these, however, had gone on at day-break to the night's resting-place after the first day's march.

At Haider Pasha an immense number of peo-

ple had assembled, of whom more than the half
wore yashmaks. The Sultan himself was in his
kioshk.   Here prayers and other ceremonies
having been performed, the troops manœuvred
and marched past, and the caravan again put
itself in motion.*   At this parting point it was
not very numerous, but like a school-boy's snow-
ball " vires acquirit eundo ;" and it is always
stated to enter Mekkah seventy thousand strong;
for if it does not really consist of so great a
number of mortals, the deficiency is supplied
by the requisite number of invisible angels.

* On the night preceding the departure of the caravan,
all the men-of-war in harbour, and all the mosques,
were illuminated, the minarets of the latter being connected by festoons of lamps. The night was dark,
but clear and serene, and the effect produced by this
blaze of light, as seen from our windows, was extremely beautiful and brilliant.

It is a known fact that many incurable in-
valids, and decrepid old men—many, in fact,
who are aware that they have but few months,
or even days, to live, undertake this hajj, in the
hope of dying on the road, in which case they
are sure of obtaining admittance to heaven.
Their hopes, however, are not always fulfilled,
for an old man who kept a shop in the Serej
bazaar, told me that with this view he had
twice performed the hajj, but had returned, not
only with life, but with re-established health
and vigour.

As we are now on the other side of the
water, I may as well say a few words of Iskiudar, or Scutari. This town was the ancient
Chrysopolis, and on the heights above it was
fought the decisive battle between Constantine
and Licinius, which insured to the former the
undisputed possession of the empire.   It is very

prettily situated, and has some wide streets,
but no very remarkable buildings. The
principal of these are the large and extensive infantry barracks, which form so conspicuous a feature in the landscape; the
cavalry barracks of Top-tash, and the mosque
of Selim III., which is simple, but in very
good taste.* There is also another mosque
built in 954 of the Hejra, by the Princess
Mihrumah, daughter of Sultan Suleyman I.,
with others of less note; and close to the water

* We entered this mosque without even taking off
our boots, and were followed by a great number of
soldiers just dismissed from parade, who seemed to
vie with each other in doing the honours of the place,
showing us all its different parts, and pointing out
their several uses; and whenever we said anything in
admiration, they appeared exceedingly delighted.

is a small serai belonging to the Sultan, called
Shums kioshk, or Pavilion of the Sun.

Iskiudar also contained the printing office established by Selim III. This monarch was
not, however, as is generally supposed, the first
who introduced typography into the Othmanlu
empire. Its first appearance was made as far
back as the reign of Ahmed III. in 1139 H.
(A.D. 1726,) under the direction and super-
intendence of Ibrahim Efendi, a man of great
learning and talents, and of Seid Efendi. The
first work issued from this press was the Ketab
Loghat Wankooli, in two volumes, folio. After
the death of Ibrahim in 1170, no other books
appear to have been published till printing was
revived by Sultan Abd-ul-hameed.

Off Iskiudar is a small rock, on which has
been built a tower and a saluting battery. It
is called by the Christians, Leander's Tower,

for what reason, it is impossible to say; the
Turks calls it Kiz-koulleh, (the Maiden's
Tower,) and a very romantic story is related
by them of a princess who was confined in it,
and her lover, a young Irani.

A ride should be taken from Scutari to the
summit of the hill of Bourgurlu, from which a
very extensive view is obtained of the country:
Stambool, Iskiudar, Kadi-keui, Pera, the Bosphorus, the Kara-deniz, or Black Sea, the Sea
of Marmora, the Prince's Islands, the snowy
Olympus, or Cheshish Dagh, and many of the
hills and valleys of Anadoly. The road is
partly paved, and passes by a small villa built
by Selim for his mother, and between Bourgurlu and Janileji, where the Sultan has a
house.

On returning one day, we turned to the left,
passing by another small country-house of the

Sultan's, opposite which are seen a variety of small marble columns, commemorating the distance of some of his shots. Before us lay the pretty point of Fanari-baghcheh, with the Sultan's serai embosomed in groves, and the town of Kadi-keui, formerly *Chalcedonia.* Between these is Moundeh-bourun.

At Fanari-baghcheh are seen the remains of Justinian's villa and baths. The point itself is the *Hereum prom.,* and the bay the *Portus Eutropius.* At Kadi-keui I did not observe any thing worthy of notice, except, perhaps, what remains of the church of St. Eufemia. Between Kadi-keui and Iskiudar, and close to Kaoak-serai, is the fountain of Hermagora.

The number of palaces and kioshks belonging to the Sultan in the immediate neighbourhood of the capital is very great. I know of the following, and probably many others exist.

The winter and summer palaces of the Seraglio ;
the Eski-serai, Galata-serai, and two at Eyoob ;
Beshik-tash, Dolmah-baghcheh, Bebek, Therapia, Sweet Waters of Asia, Stavros, Che-
raghan, Beglerbeg, Shums-serai, Kandelli,
Bourgurlu, Jamleji, Yldiz kioshk, St. Stefano,
Biuyuk Chekmejji, Daood Pasha, Fanari-
baghcheh, Ok Meidan, Kaoak-serai, Haider
Pasha, and Kiaghd-khaneh. Some of these are,
however, merely small summer villas, where he
only spends a day or two, or perhaps only a
few hours.

The rides about Stambool are quite delightful—beautiful views on all sides, a fine turf,
and an unenclosed country, cannot but make
them so. About the Ok-Meidan, the Sweet
Waters, and Ramas Chiftlek, the turf is especially good, equalling in goodness the best kept
English lawn.

The ride to Daood Pasha is very pretty—
one may gallop the whole way, if mounted on a
good Turkish horse, and not afraid to venture
down one or two ravines of steep broken
ground. Keeping along the heights, you proceed to the top of the Golden Horn, and then
descend into the rich and verdant valley of the
Sweet Waters. Here stands one of the imperial palaces, a building formerly used as a
paper manufactory ; it is surrounded by fine
large trees, and in part overhangs the Kiaghd-
khaneh-su, *(Barbysses,)* whose banks are cased
with stone, and whose waters are made to form
a very pretty little cascade.

The meadows on both sides are favourite resorts with parties of pleasure and pic-nics, and
here on festivals are seen mingled in one society
the Turkish flowers of the harem, in their
snowy yashmaks and yellow slippers,—Grecian

beauties, with unveiled faces and sandalled
shoes,—purple-booted Armenians, and black-
booted Jewesses; and with a proper proportion
of the male members of these respective sects,
in their gay and splendid costumes, they form
a brilliant *coup d'œil.*

Many additional trees have lately been
planted in these meadows, which in a few
years will render them still more delightful.
About the end of April, the greater part of the
Sultan's horses are turned into them to grass for
the summer.

Ascending the stream is Kiaghd-khaneh-
keui, a small village, where Mons. Roger, secretary of the French embassy, and son-in-law
of General Guilleminot, used to keep a small
pack of hounds, with whom we often went out,
and had several good runs, especially when we
had a wolf a-head; these animals always took

us a long run to the Forest of Belighrad.   On
the adjoining downs I have often met the Sultan's greyhounds coursing; they are large dogs,
of a light cream colour, and have a tuft of
hair at the end of the tail, like what we see
on lions.   They are covered with very warm
body clothes, even when the weather is not very
cold.

Soon after leaving the Kiaghd-khaneh-su,
you cross another stream, called at present the
Mahklena, (formerly the *Cydaris*,) both flowing into the Golden Horn; and then ascend
the heights on which stand the large barracks*
of Ramas Chiftlek, perhaps the most conspicuous
object round Stambool.   Near these is a spot

* The new Turkish barracks are all built according
to one plan, forming a large hollow square, with
square towers at each angle, surmounted by high conical roofs like our church steeples.

from which a beautiful and extensive view is
obtained, looking down the whole length of the
harbour.   •

Opposite the barracks, and fronting inland,
are some lines strengthened at intervals by batteries, thrown up during the last war to cover
the capital from the Russians, and behind them,
the Sultan with from fifteen to twenty thousand
men were encamped.   The country in front is
open, free from wood, and forming a succession
of ridges and valleys resembling some parts of
Picardy and Champagne.   A little beyond is
the large military hospital, called Maldepeh,
from its proximity to the mound already mentioned as the one on which Muhammed II.
planted his standard during the siege of Stambool.   Between this and Daood Pasha is a
small fountain, evidently of ancient construction, although a Turkish inscription has been
carved upon it.

The barracks of Daood Pasha are built on the site of some ancient palace, or monastery. At the time of one of our visits, the first, or se-rasker's regiment of infantry, was quartered here, under the command of Noorid Bey, a very intelligent officer, who was extremely civil, and gave me many details respecting the new army of Turkey. he spoke French very tolerably. The regiment turned out, and went through a very good field-day on the downs. I particularly remarked the perfect correctness of distances and covering in column.

Close by is a villa belonging to the Sultan, who has also a quarter in the barracks.

Other rides may be made to the ruined barracks of Sevend Chiftlek, to Belighrad, to Domuz-dereh, to Biuyuk-dereh, — but it is needless to specify them all, as the country being quite open, you are at liberty to put your

horse's head in any direction your fancy may
point out.

The ride by the lower road to Therapia is
also extremely pretty, passing through the numerous villages which line the European shore
of the Bosphorus.   I had long been inquiring,
but always in vain, for the tomb of that scourge
and terror of Christians, the famous Barbarossa;
when one day, as I was lounging through
these different villages, I observed in that
of Beshik-tash an octangular building, surmounted by a dome, and on reading the inscription over the door, I found that I had now
by chance discovered what I had long been in
search of.   It stated, that this building was the
turbeh, or tomb, " of the conqueror of Algiers
and of Tunis, the fervent Islam soldier of God,
the Capudan Khair-ed-Deen, (Barbarossa,) upon
whom may the protection of God repose." It bears

the date of 948 H.; but as this does not agree with
the year of his death, which was later, it probably refers to the time of its erection by Barbarossa previous to his death. On most Turkish
buildings are chronological inscriptions which
give the date of its erection, if not otherwise
stated in numbers. Thus, for example,
محمد رسول الله, a well-known part of the article of faith would represent the date 454; viz.
M. 40; H. 8; M. 40; D. 4; R. 200; S. 60;
U. 6; L. 30; A. 1; L L. 60; soft H. 5.
I do not, however, mean it to be understood
that these sacred words are ever employed in
this manner; I have only instanced them as
the first that presented themselves.

In the interior of Barbarossa's tomb are four
coffins; over his own floats a large green silk
flag with sentences from the Koran in white
letters, the famous double-bladed sword called

Zulfecar, and the names of the Prophet, Omar, Aboobeker, Othman, and Ali; these names, with " Allah," are often united in the following curious monogram.

CHAPTER XIII.

A Ball at the Ambassador's—The Seraglio Library—
The Baghdah Palace—St. Irene—The Mint—Sar-
cophagi — Bazaars — Bezesteens — Khans — Slave
Market.

On the 22nd of January, one of the Oda-
leks presented the Sultan with a young princess, named Khair Allah. This event was
announced to the capital by the batteries and
the men-of-war dressed out with flags, firing
salutes three times a day for three successive
days; had it been a prince the salutes would
have continued nine days.

On the 25th our ambassador gave a grand
ball in the Palace of England, at which all the

great Turkish dignitaries were present ; and
it was even supposed that the Sultan himself
would have looked in.   The grandees consisted
of the Reis Efendi Ahmed Hameed Bey, Halil
Capudan Pasha, the Serasker Hosrew Mehemmed, the Selihtar, Ahmed Pasha of the
Bosphorus, Tahir Pasha, general-in-chief of the
artillery, (who commanded the navy at Navarin,) Abdny Bey, and several other officers.

The band of the guards, composed entirely
of young Turks, played quadrilles, valtzes,
cotillons, &c.   The ball commenced by their
playing the sultan's march, after which a polo-
naise was danced, the serasker opening the procession with the French ambassadress, the Capudan Pasha following with Lady Temple, and
the Selihtar Agha with Madame l'Internonce
of Austria.   Lady Temple also valtzed with
Ahmed Pasha and Abdny Bey.   A room fitted
up with divans was allotted to smoking.

During supper the precepts of the Koran did not for the moment appear to be uppermost in the minds of the Othmanlus, the contents of the Champagne and Bourdeaux bottles vanishing with incredible celerity.   They perhaps thought that as the Koran promises to the faithful the unlimited use of wine in the next world,* it could be no very great sin if they allowed themselves to take a little *à compte* in this.   The party did not retire till a late hour, and seemed highly delighted with the *fête.*

* In the fifty-sixth chapter of the Koran, called the Judgment, it is particularly and clearly stated that among other rewards prepared for the elect, "they will be waited upon by children possessed of everlasting youth, who will offer them the most exquisite wines in cups of various forms.   The fumes of the wine will not mount to their heads, and will not obscure their reason."

Some days after, the French ambassador gave a ball, at which the Turkish ministers assisted. At this rather an awkward mistake occurred. Orders had been given that no Turkish servants should have access to the vicinity of the state apartments, but that they were to be entertained in a separate part of the palace. The Reis Efendi, or minister for foreign affairs, who always dresses with remarkable plainness and simplicity, upon riding up to the entrance, was mistaken by the ambassador's servants for one of the suite of some Turkish nobleman, and refused admittance, notwithstanding the asseverations of the great man that he was Reis Efendi, a *ministro*,—the liveried gentry thinking all the time that he merely meant that he formed one of that personage's suite. In a furious rage Ahmed Hameed turned his horse, and was riding away, when fortunately one of the French attachés, drawn to the spot by the noise of the discussion, perceived the mistake, and running after the minister, succeeded by many apologies in calming him. General Guilleminot, who had in the mean time been informed of the affair, instantly came out, and with his polite and engaging manners, soon caused the affront to be forgotten, and entering the ball-room with the Reis Efendi, nothing farther occurred to interrupt the gaiety of the evening.

Sir Robert Gordon during the winter gave many other balls and parties, as did also the French and Austrian ambassadors.

Nothing could equal Sir Robert Gordon's kindness to ourselves during the whole period of our stay at Stambool. He offered us apartments in the palace; fitted up our house with furniture; his servants, horses, and kaeeks

were at our disposal, and every day he invited
us to dine at the palace, sending a sedan-chair*
for Lady Temple.

On twelfth-day we went to a party at Mr.
Cartwright's, our consul-general, to draw the
bean, and here we witnessed the performances
of Kara-kooz, (black-eyes,) the Turkish pulci-
nella. The room being darkened, a white sheet
is drawn across a part of it, having a strong
light behind; the actors, cut out of camel's
skin, are moved by sticks, the little figures

* The bearers of the sedan-chair had a peculiar
costume, consisting of a large sable-fur cap, like those
worn by the dragomanerie, scarlet benishes, or long
frock-coats, and yellow Morocco boots.

The arrival of an ambassador on a visit, or at a
party, is announced by a large bell being tolled three
times, that of a minister by two pulls, and that of
other individuals by one.

being laid close to the sheet. Much wit and
many jokes were uttered, but they required
the audience to be perfectly *au fait* to Turkish
idioms to be fully relished. The little vaude-
ville, if we may so call it, which we saw acted,
represented the adventures of Kara-kooz at one
of the Beiram festivals.

As I before mentioned, leave had been granted
me to enter the seraglio whenever I pleased, in
order to see the cavalry regiments of the guard,
who were quartered there. Without this permission no one is allowed to penetrate beyond
the first court. These regiments used to be
drilled twice a week by Colonel Calosso, whom
I accompanied on some of these occasions,
taking a boat at Topkhaneh, and landing at the
little kioshk, where disgraced vizeers are usually
beheaded—behind which is a little door which
gives admittance within the walls of the seraglio,

close to the cavalry barracks. After spending
some time with the officers, and attending the
drills, Colonel Calosso used to take me over the
different parts of the seraglio. In this manner
I saw the whole of it, the women's quarters of
course excepted.

It is not my intention minutely to describe
the seraglio. Tavernier has given so detailed
an account of it as to have filled no less than
ninety folio pages; and though I have never
read his work, I have heard it spoken of as
being correct. Dr. Clarke has also given a
minute description of it, chiefly taken, as I have
heard, either from Tavernier, or from the rela-
tions given him by the officers and servants of the
palace. As to his having himself gone over the
interior, it has generally been doubted, and by
many have I heard it positively denied.

Muhammed II. is said to have added to the

seraglio seventy royal and private apartments. The harem was built by Suleyman I., who also made several other additions.

The famous library, (an octagonal and insulated building, resembling Suleyman's turbeh,) is supposed to contain many literary treasures. It is not, however, kept in good order, or, more properly speaking, it is probably seldom or never opened; the dust, in consequence, has accumulated to a great degree on the volumes, which are laid horizontally on shelves. Several panes of glass were also broken, which gave admittance to some pigeons, one of whose nests I observed comfortably arranged among the books. I could hear nothing of the existence of a catalogue, and the librarian did not in the least seem inclined to allow me to make one, had I been disposed to do so, which I must candidly confess I was not; for though the number of volumes was not very great, yet the task of looking them over seemed likely to prove neither short nor easy. On my asking him what scarce works it contained, he answered, "that God knew;" to which assertion I could not do otherwise than assent, and appear to be satisfied with.

The Baghdad palace, erected by Murad IV. pleased me much: it is richly decorated with marbles of every variety, with soft Persian carpets, divans of silk and velvet, porcelain tiles, gilding, inscriptions, arms, &c. The number of ancient marble columns and pillars in the different palaces and kioshks is very great; and in a yard adjoining the winter-harem, I observed a very fine altar of porphyry, at present used as the pedestal of a sun-dial. Nothing can equal the richness and beauty of design of the arabesque ornaments which adorn the ceilings of the rooms, the gates, the porticos, and the under part of the far-projecting eaves of the different buildings. Gold and vivid colours are mingled in every possible variety of pattern, but always with good taste, and in good keeping. The chapel in which the ceremony of blessing the presents to the shrine of Mekkah takes place, is very handsome.

The old church of St. Irene once contained a valuable collection of eastern arms, which are now lodged in the treasury, where may also be seen huge chests, said to contain incalculable wealth. The Sultan would doubtless be delighted to find that such indeed were the case.

The mint is well worthy of inspection, and the work done is very good, of which I obtained a proof in a rich sword-scabbard which I had made there. It was ornamented with sentences from the Koran, flowers, &c. all in high relief;

and the workmanship was such, that though perhaps it may be equalled in London or Paris, it certainly cannot be excelled.

The hall where the new ambassadors and ministers dine before being presented to the Sultan, and the hall of audience, or Arz Oda, have often, I believe, been described; for, when any foreign diplomatic personage is first presented, he has the privilege of taking with him, not only all the subjects of his sovereign, but even some of those of other powers, so that many persons have had opportunities of seeing these apartments. There is a collection of the portraits of the sultans, some of which I had copied. The stables "resemble those of Antar." The kitchens are large and numerous, each surmounted by a small cupola. They are not quite arranged according to a French *artiste's* taste, for few are the *fourneaux* and the *casseroles*, but in their place are large fires and enormous cauldrons. The consumption of provisions must necessarily be great ; in some work I have seen them stated at a hundred and ten oxen, two hundred sheep, one hundred lambs or kids, ten calves, two hundred fowls, four hundred pullets, two hundred pigeons, and fifty geese daily, besides game ; and, if the accounts of Turkish writers are correct, (who state that forty thousand souls were formerly lodged within the walls of the seraglio,) the number probably is not overrated, great as it appears. The Turks are renowned for their knowledge in the science of cookery, and as far as I have been able to judge, deservedly so.

The great hammams are large and handsome, and of white marble, and are kept heated till twelve o'clock every day. I found them filled with officers and pages, either bathing or

L 5

making their toilettes. I was much amused at
seeing one of the latter busily employed in
starching his shirt,—he did not seem quite
au fait to the undertaking, for he was laying
large handfuls over every part of it.

There are three odas of Aech oghlans, or
pages, a corps from which most of the officers
are taken. These rooms are long, with a gallery running round the top, and supported by
gilt pillars, carved in imitation of palm-trees;
the rooms also have a profusion of gilding,
painting, &c., resembling the style prevalent
during the reign of Louis XIV. Attached to
each oda is a café, or mess-room, and a bath.
We paid visits to each, and were most warmly
received, for Rustam Bey is a general favourite.
In these assemblies, we not only met the pages,
but military and civil officers of rank, and with
them we smoked, drank coffee, and chatted,

and with difficulty escaped making several din-
ners, for numerous were the invitations to stop
and eat, " *Aghaler, bir lokmah shi eyehlum.*"
They all seemed very anxious to hear news,
especially as to the prospects of war or peace ;
for after the usual salutations of " *Khosh gel-
danuz—Khosh bolduk, efendim,*" " You are
welcome, you are well met, sir !" the invariable
questions were, " *Neh kbaber,*" " What news ?"
" *Bir khaberin yokmi ?*" " Do you know any
news ?"

I certainly did not remark, on these and the
like occasions, where all ceremony was dis-
carded, that the Turks are a more silent race
than other nations, nor did they have recourse
to the state of the weather to nourish a conver-
sation ; never have I been told that the day
was a fine or a bad one, at times when the ob-
servation was so self-evident as to require no
remark.

Within the walls of the seraglio is a deer
park, and several very pretty and well-kept
flower-gardens, with fountains, swings, and
round-abouts.   Evliya describes them as
being " delightful as the gardens of Irem,
planted with twenty thousand cypress-trees, and
many hundred thousand fruit-trees, forming an
aviary and tulip-bed only comparable to the
gardens of the genii."

The summer-harem is at the Seraglio Point,
close to the water ; however, in passing near
either this or the winter one, never were my
eyes rewarded by the sight of any lovely sultana or odalek, though I looked up atten-
tively at every latticed window in the hopes of
beholding some of those brilliant orbs, compared to which the eyes of the ghazal and
zareef are said to be but lifeless clay. No
floral *billet* was dropped in my path—no

old woman pulled my sleeve; not the shadow
of a romantic adventure have I to record—unfortunate giaour that I am !*

The sultan's sister is frequently to be met
driving about even in the streets of infidel Pera,
and she is by no means particular about keeping her yashmak over her face : she has even
been known to stop and speak to Christians. For
this extraordinary sort of conduct she is looked
upon by the Turks as afflicted with insanity.

There are in Stambool two sarcophagi, both
supposed to have contained the ashes of Constantine, the founder of the city.   One of them

* It is well known that the language of flowers
originated with the inmates of the Turkish harems ;
it is, however, not solely confined to flowers, but
extends to fruits and other objects ; a pear, for instance, signifying " Give me some hope,"—a thread,
" Faithful to thee even in absence."

stands in a little square near the Seirek, or
Monasteer Jamaa—it is of a fine green brescia,
resembling *verd' antico*, and is at present used
as a reservoir of water. The Turks call it
Kostantin Mezar. The other one, which is of
red porphyry, stands in the court of the mosque
called Noor Othmanieh. I feel inclined to look
upon this latter as the true one, for if I mistake
not, historians have stated that the emperor's
body, having been placed in a gold coffin, was
deposited in a sarcophagus of porphyry. I do
not, however, speak with certainty, as I have
no book by me to refer to.

The most amusing lounges to a stranger are
decidedly the bazaars, bezesteens, and khans.
Entering the former for the first time, you
fancy yourself in a dark and very complicated
labyrinth, crowded to excess by persons of all nations, busily trying, some to extricate themselves

from its mazes, others to penetrate still further
into them; whilst the cries of persons walking
up and down offering their goods for sale—
the bargaining on all sides—the shouts of the
shopkeepers calling back some person to say
that they accept his offer—the cries of the
guards and servants who clear the way for some
Turkish grandee advancing at a quick pace
on a spirited charger,—combine to render the
scene as noisy as it is animated. Then, as
you pass the different shops, you are invited to
purchase, " *Gel, Efendim, bir shi lazem mi?*"
" Come here, Efendi, what do you wish for?"
" *Soilniz neh estersiz, ia Agha!*" " Tell me
what you want, O Agha!"

A purchase is not so easily effected as might
be imagined; and unless you determine to
pay at once what is asked, much squabbling
and time is required to make a bargain. As,

however, all the different trades have distinct
quarters, the shops selling the same sort of
goods are close together, so that you have
only to go from one to the other till you have
suited yourself. When the bargain is concluded, the merchant generally tells you that
he has only gained a few paras, or, perhaps,
nothing at all, adding, " *Ai ! ai ! neh eoileh
pek adem siz—Amer Allaheen !*" " Ai ! ai !
what a difficult man you are to deal with—but
God's will be done !"

I strongly recommend all persons to confine
their dealings as much as possible to Turks,
who are easily known by their white turbans;
they possess better goods, are incalculably
more honest, and do not importune you. Next
to them apply to the Armenians, and, if you
can avoid it, have nothing whatever to say to
Greeks or Jews ;—I say, if you can avoid it,

because these two latter classes are precisely
those who rush round you, overwhelm you
with civil speeches, tell countless lies, and,
speaking a little Italian, finally succeed in
drawing the bewildered traveller into their
stalls and plundering him.   I have often heard
Christian merchants who have long been in the
habit of trading with the Turks, say, that they
relied as much on the *word* of a Moslem as on
the *bond* of one of themselves.   Lord Byron,
who, from his knowledge of the East, must be
considered good authority on this subject, says,
that " in all transactions with the Moslems, I
ever found the strictest honour, the highest dis-
interestedness.   In transacting business with
them, there are none of those dirty peculations,
under the name of interest, difference of exchange, commission, &c., uniformly found in
applying to a Greek house to cash bills, even
on the first in Pera."

One of the shops best known to English travellers is that kept by Hajji Mustafa, who was
formerly a page in the seraglio, and in whose
shop the Sultan takes his place during the festi-
val of the Beyram, to see what passes. Mustafa sells his goods very dear, but they are certainly far better than what can be obtained anywhere else; besides which, he invites you into
his interior room, where you are served with
narghilehs, chibooks, coffee, sherbet, sweetmeats,
and your hands, mustachios, and handkerchief,
are sprinkled with a variety of perfumes—and
all this to a new-arrival is pleasant enough.

The shopkeepers do not live in the bazaars,
but retire to their respective homes at three
o'clock, at which time the bazaars are shut; by
that hour the motley assembly of Turks,
Syrians, Egyptians, Abyssinians, Negroes,
Manghrebeens, Armenians, Bulgarians, Jews,

Greeks, Crimeans, Turkomans, and Franks, have all passed away, and no one is seen through the deserted passage but a solitary sentry, or a lean dog seeking for a scanty meal; whilst the quays along the harbour are crowded with Franks, Armenians, and Greeks, about to embark in kaeeks for Galata.

The bazaar of stationery, and where the writing of books, &c. is carried on, is a little beyond the Eski Serai—the books are, however, sold in the large bazaar.

The Serej, or sadlery bazaar, is near the Marcian column; and a little farther on, is the At, or horse bazaar, which is well worth visiting; the horse-dealers' stables are all in its immediate vicinity.

There are two bezesteens, one for silks, the other for arms, and every variety of second-hand things. Here I picked up some very

curious arms of different sorts.   These places
close at twelve o'clock.

The khans are buildings erected by different
sultans, or by wealthy individuals, for the re-
ception of travelling merchants and their goods.
They are large stone edifices, and have iron
doors and shutters to guard against fire.
Almost all of them are endowed, consequently only a very trifling sum is paid for
the rooms.   They are generally three or
four stories high, and in them the merchant
finds himself and his bales in perfect security
from both fire and popular commotions.   Some
of them are of great size, surrounding a court
in which are trees, fountains, *cafés*, and stables.
It is stated that there exist no less than one
hundred and ninety of these establishments in
Stambool, the largest of which. is the Valideh
khan.   This was originally the serai of Jarrah

Muhammed Pasha, but was afterwards almost
entirely rebuilt by the Valideh Khoseem, mother of Murad IV. It contains a mosque,
three hundred rooms, and, originally, had sta-
bling for one thousand horses.

Those persons who intend to make large
purchases, and wish to see the best articles,
must not fail to visit these places, where they
will find the greatest varieties of the fine-
textured muslins of India, the softest and
richest shawls of Tabreez and of Kushmeer,
tne gay carpets of Persia, the flowered silks of
the East, the beautiful skins of the samoor
and the black fox, and large quantities of
pearls, brilliants, and other precious stones.
Here, also, are occasionally to be met with, the
costly effects of exiled or beheaded pashas.

We ought now to notice another species of
bazaar, different from the others, but at the

same time very interesting,—I mean the slave-
market, (Asir khan,) established by Beiram
Pasha, vizeer of Murad IV.* It is situated
near the burnt column. The *locale* has nothing
very remarkable about it, being an open space
surrounded by small buildings, with covered
galleries in front; in the centre are some similar
buildings; the black men, women, and children, and some of the commoner white ones, are
seated either in the galleries or in the open air,
in different groups, forming the property of
their respective owners.

Judging from the sounds of laughter, and
from the broad grins displaying beautiful rows
of pearl-white teeth, these slaves, whom it is so
much the custom to pity, appeared very contented and happy, or rather, seemed looking
forward with certainty to their being so when

* The *penjek,* or duty on captives, is paid here.

purchased—for there is not the slightest doubt
that, generally speaking, the slaves in Turkey
are as happy and contented as any other class
of the community : they are well fed, clothed,
treated, and educated, by their masters, and
in their old age are not abandoned.* The
women, if pretty, or possessed of the art of
pleasing, lead a luxurious and voluptuous life,
whilst to the men the highest offices of the
state are open—witness the present serasker,
the Capudan Pasha about to marry the Sultan's
daughter, Mustafa Efendi, the chief secretary'
e tanti altri.

It may here be remarked, that one of the
most remarkable features in the Turkish cha-

* My observations on the happy state of slaves are
made only in reference to those in the Turkish dominions ;—as to what their condition is under Christian
lords, let the negroes of the Brazils, the United States,
and the West Indies, speak.

racter is the natural dignity they all possess, which qualifies them to bear with such graceful ease the high offices so often and so suddenly conferred on members of the very lowest classes. A man to-day is a vizeer or a pasha, who but the day before was a porter or a boatman; and yet after watching him closely, you feel inclined to believe, from his manners and bearing, that during the whole of his life he has held the highest rank in society, and not only so, but that his family have done so for successive generations before him.

The fair flowers of Georgia, of Circassia, and of Greece, being of much greater value than the rest, and being reserved for the Sultan or his pashas, are not exposed to the vulgar gaze, but are kept within doors.—The Turks, for some time after the conclusion of the peace, were in great alarm lest (the Russians being in possession of the ports of the Black Sea, from which these lovely objects are exported,) the trade should cease. The love of gold was, however, stronger than religious principle, and the Christian Russians have already sent several cargoes of these precious wares to the bazaars of Stambool.

CHAPTER XIV.

Galata—Pera—Topkhaneh—Over-land passage of the
Fleet of Muhammed II.—Gibbon's Doubts—Statements of Saeed-ed-Deen and Evliya Efendi—Praises
of Constantinople—Return to Naples.

GALATA, in my opinion, is a detestable place.
Off its quays the merchant-ships are anchored
in three or four rows; the streets are filled
with drinking houses for the numerous Frank
and Greek sailors, and are dirty, and the
shops are of a very inferior description. All
the Christian merchants have their banks and
stores here, though they themselves mostly live
at Pera. The place is surrounded by a wall
strengthened by towers, and on different parts

of them are seen Latin inscriptions of the middle ages, and coats of arms carved on marble. It contains a considerable number of large, substantially-built brick houses, of the time of the Genoese, whose Hotel de Ville is still standing. The Arab Jamaa, formerly a church of the Dominicans, is the only curious one.

Pera is a suburb of Galata, and contains all the palaces of the different embassies and legations—the largest and handsomest is that of England, built during the time of Lord Elgin; it has also the advantage of being isolated, and surrounded on all sides by a large garden, so that in the event of a plague or a fire breaking out, the inmates are in almost perfect safety. On the summit is a *Belvedere,* from which a beautiful and extensive view is obtained. The rooms are large and handsome, especially the state, or ball-room.

M 2

Next to this in appearance is that of France;
then come those of Austria, (formerly the palace of the Venetian republic, and built of
wood,) and of Holland. The others are not
deserving of the name of palaces.

The other buildings of any note are, the
Galata Serai, where a number of Aech Oghlans
are educated; the Greek church, which is very
handsomely decorated; the Tekkeh of the
Derwishes; and the large barracks at the end
of the street, and overlooking the Bosphorus.

Topkhaneh, another suburb, contains the
fine artillery arsenal, from which it takes its
name, and a cannon foundery. The mosque attached to the arsenal is very handsome, and
differs in many points from the style of archi-
tecture usually adopted in these buildings. In
the centre of the square in front, is a splendid fountain, the number and richness of whose

decorations and inscriptions is really astonishing : it is of the same form as the one opposite
the Bab Humayoom, but considerably larger ;
the gilding and colours are not, however, nearly
so fresh and vivid.

The famous Capudan Pasha, surnamed by
the Christians, Mezzomorto, also built a palace
and a mosque in this quarter. Being about
sailing in command of a fleet, he left directions
as to plans and elevations, but on returning, it
is related, that not pleased with the appearance
of these edifices, he laid his ships along-side,
and knocked them to pieces with his cannon.
The reigning sultan, however, ordered him immediately to re-construct them. Such, at
least, is the story told by the kaeekjis.

Dolma-baghcheh Iskelleh is the place where
Muhammed II., unable to break through the
chain drawn across the mouth of the Golden

Horn, landed his fleet, and by means of a well-
greased road of planks, and aided by the exer-
tions of his sailors, and of part of his army,
conveyed it in one single night up the valley to
the summit of the heights near the Armenian
burial-ground, and thence down the opposite
one to Terskhaneh ; where he again launched it
in the morning, to the utter dismay and astonishment of the Christians, who had up to this
moment been kept in high spirits by an old
prophecy, which asserted that Constantinople
never could be taken unless a hostile king
could make his ships pass over the land with
their sails set. On the appearance, therefore,
of the Turkish ships advancing across the neck
of land to attack them, it is but natural to
suppose that their livers turned to water.

Gibbon places the scene of the landing of
the ships at Balta-liman, and, on that sup-

position, doubts the whole fact. Turkish
historians have, perhaps, in some instances
wished, by increasing the distance, to add to
the greatness of the enterprise. Saeed-ed-
Deen says, that "the conqueror of the world
conceived the design of conveying the Moslem
ships from the fortress which had been built,
to the port behind Galata." By "the fortress
which had been built," we naturally suppose that the still-existing castle, called Rou-
mili Hissar, is the place alluded to, though
in this case the distance would still be very
great. But is there any proof that no fortifica-
tion was constructed by the Turks at Dolma-
baghcheh, which may since have been pulled
down? What we positively do know is, that
the Turkish fleet was conveyed over land from
some part of the Bosphorus to the Golden Horn,
and that Dolma-baghcheh is the point where

the undertaking could the most easily have been performed.

Evliya Efendi gives another version: he says, that Muhammed ordered Timur-tash Pasha, and two thousand soldiers, to construct at Kiaghd-khaneh, fifty kadirghehs or galleys, and Kojah Mustafa Pasha, with his Arabs, to build fifty galleys, and fifty horse-boats at Levend Chiftlek, and that this order was carried into execution; Mustafa, conveying his vessels on rollers and greased planks along the land, and launching them at Shah-kuli-iskelleh under the Ok-Meidan, whilst Timur, I suppose, launched his quite at the head of the harbour.

I cannot quit old Stambool without expressing my astonishment that so lovely a spot should so seldom have been visited by travellers: within the last few years, I do not suppose that the number exceeds ten or twelve:

yearly. Whether this proceeds from a want
of curiosity, or is occasioned by an idea of the
difficulties attending such an excursion, or by
a consideration of its distance, I do not know.
If the latter, I can only state that it is much
easier to go to Constantinople than to Vienna;
the packet takes the traveller to Malta, from
which vessels sail weekly to the capital of the
Othman Empire. Perhaps some may have been
terrified by the accounts of certain old writers,
who lead one to expect nothing in Turkey but
a succession of misfortunes and horrors. According to these, plague, pestilence, famine,
fire, massacres, bastinadoes, imprisonments, in-
sults, want of water, are evils of daily occurrence. Now, on the contrary, judging from
what I observed myself, and from what I heard
on the spot, I should say that there is not
anywhere a more delightful and healthy cli-

M 5

mate than is to be found at Stambool and its
environs. As a proof of this, I need only mention that several Frank medical men have
lately quitted it, *faute de malades;* the plague
has not raged to any extent since 1812; and,
in 1830, when this malady, united with the
cholera, ravaged the neighbouring territories
of Persia, Russia, and the principalities, Stambool remained perfectly free and clear from
them, and that not owing to quarantine and
sanitary laws, (for none exist,) but solely to
the natural purity of the climate. Heat and
cold are never felt in great extremes, and a
constant current of air is produced by the Bosphorus.

Instead of witnessing frequent and extensive
fires, we only saw a single and very trifling one,
which was immediately extinguished by the
troops and tuloombajis, all the guard-houses

being provided with fire-engines. I must here state, that after a fire the Sultan furnishes the sufferers with lodging, or causes a sufficient number of tents to be issued out for their use. Carpenters, masons, &c., are prohibited, under severe penalties, from asking more in rebuilding the houses than the regular rate of wages; and the price of wood and other materials is fixed, and cannot exceed what it was before the fire.

As for riots, murders, or executions, I neither saw nor heard of any. No heads were to be seen at the Bab Humayoom, nor headless trunks at the Four Corners. That each and all of these *désagrémens* have taken place, I do not however mean to deny, but certainly now they are of very rare occurrence.

Provisions are good, plentiful, and cheap. Some of the wines are good, especially that of

Tenedos. Riding, hunting, coursing, shooting, fishing,* and sailing, can all be enjoyed in perfection. Wild boar, red deer, chevreuil, hares, partridges, pheasants, woodcock, snipe, and wild fowl, abound in the immediate neighbourhood.

Perhaps one of the reasons why game is so plentiful in Turkey, is that the Mussulmen have rather a repugnance to eat it. Why, I know not; for the Koran, in the fifth chapter, only forbids game being killed and eaten during the pilgrimage to Mekkah. In a few verses further on in the same chapter, it is positively stated, that " when the pilgrimage is accomplished, hunting is permitted." And again: " The prey, which animals killed by

---

* Fishing by torch-light in quiet summer evenings in the Bosphorus, is a great amusement with the Turkish, Armenian, and Greek women.

hunting, according to the laws received from God, may afford you, is allowed."

The beauty of the country is enchanting and unequalled. The people are honest, kind, and obliging. Lord Byron states, " There does not exist a more honourable, friendly, and high-spirited character, than the true Turkish agha, or Moslem private gentleman."

A yacht in these waters greatly adds to the delight of a residence at Stambool, visiting in it the Black Sea, the sea of Marmora, the Dardanelles, and the Egean, the shores of all which are very fine and full of interest—as almost every mountain, headland, valley, town, and village, is connected with the brilliant history of former days.

In short, I am more delighted with Constantinople than with any other place I have ever seen, and it was with the sincerest regret

that we left it on the 4th of February to return
to Italy.

We embarked on board the Maria, a small
Tuscan schooner, whose cabin I had engaged,
and warped out to Topkhaneh, intending to
sail early next morning. Wishing to obtain a
last view of this delightful spot, we rose early
next day, and found ourselves on deck, just as

> . . . the cock had crown, and light
> Began to clothe each Asiatic hill,
> And the mosque crescent struggled into sight.

We were, however, prevented from sailing
till the evening, and never, I thought, had
Stambool looked so lovely as it did at that time.
The sky was clear and serene, and the setting
sun shone brightly upon its lofty and swelling
domes, their numerous crescents glittering in its

parting beams like liquid gold, whilst numerous
blood-red flags fluttered in all directions. The
hills of Asia exhibited a variety of beautiful
tints, which gradually mingled and became
blended in one general soft hue of warm pur-
ple: this again momentarily grew colder and
colder, till the whole scene was wrapped in
darkness.

We remained for some time at anchor off
Gallipoli, and saw the ruins of the palace of
Ibrahim I., and the remains of Justinian's docks
and storehouses. At Sultan Kalaahsi we
stopped to show our firman, and pay the cus-
tomary toll; and then, propelled by a stiff but
favouring breeze, we soon entered the open sea,
sailing, as a late writer expresses himself, " from
the castellated shores of despotism, to the
smiling waves of the Egean, the sea of Freedom !" In spite, however, of this pretty sen-

tence, I could not avoid feeling that I was
leaving behind me honesty, safety, and protection, having in perspective during my course
over the free Egean, (so called, perhaps,
as Mrs. Ramsbottom would say in her letters,
from its pirates making free with your property,) nothing but rascals, robbers, and cut-
throats. On the evening of the 8th we were
off Cape Colonna, whence we scudded through
a heavy sea, *a secco,* or under bare poles. The
rolling was dreadful, and we could do nothing
but remain in our berths and read. On the 9th
we passed by Cerigo, Cape Matapan, and the
Sapienze, when the wind changed against us.
On the 13th we were near Syracuse, and doubled
Cape Passaro, not far from which we saw a large
ship on shore, which we afterwards learned was
a transport that had sailed from Malta with
part of the ninetieth regiment. Next day we

entered the harbour of Marsamucetto, and immediately went into the Lazaretto, where we performed twenty-five days' quarantine. Captain Roberts, who had quitted Stambool a month before we did, had only arrived four days before. He had landed at Lafoniskia, or Cervi island, to obtain provisions and make sketches, and had with great difficulty escaped being murdered by the Greeks.

On the 10th of March we were liberated, and embarked the same day on board the government schooner "Lady Emily," Captain Heppingstall. On the 12th we landed at Messina, and went to the opera, and on the 16th were at Naples.

This latter part of the voyage may be summed up in the following lines of Ovid:—

. . . . . Siculique angusta Pelori,
Hippotadæque domos regis, Temeseque metalla ;

Leucosiamque petit, tepidique rosaria Pœsti,

Inde legit Capreas, promontoriumque Minervæ,

Et Surrentino generosos palmite colles,

Herculeamque urbem, Stabiasque, et in otia natam

Parthenopen.

APPENDIX.

APPENDIX.

TURKISH SONGS.

I.

AIR—"HOUZAM."

Is sittim, éi rouhi gulizar
Béni guetzmesse ag-iar
Idéridim halim issar.

Nakaret.

Bou gun doursun, merakim var.

Démézmidim sana éwél,
Né soylerisse yarandirleı,
Beni dyiné, yarim sin guel :

Dussurdun sabit derdeh

Sakin sen atzma sir yerdeh,

Banah sor vakti ahardeh.

TRANSLATION.

I have heard, oh, rose-complexioned maid! and if you had not been prejudiced by my enemies, I should have been enabled to have justified myself.

Refrein.

Let it not be to-day, for I am indisposed.

Have I not before told you, that all that people said would prove false. Listen to me! Come to-morrow.

You have reduced me to an unhappy passion; but beware! mention it to no one, and apply to me at a proper time.

II.

AIR—"RARTE."

Dustu guiounum sana simdi éï péri,
Alip aklim ittin sen mahw serseri
Yoluna versem seza jan ousseri.

Nakaret.

Sevdi janim sen guibi yozma dilberi.

Bakmishé oldoun bir kevé guerdaniné,
Hali mehman ettin aldin yaniné
Ashtir atéshi brakdin januma.

Séïr idup rouhi amberin seni
Koklayanler mest olour éi meh seni
Kendiné ifdadé kildin sen beni.

TRANSLATION.

Oh, amiable love! my heart is already yours—you cause me to lose my senses—you have bewildered me. I devote myself entirely to your happiness.

Refrein.

My soul adores you exclusively, charming maid!

By having but once gazed on your neck, you have attached me, but as a wretch, and by pouring into my soul the flame of love.

They who inhale the ambered perfume of your face become intoxicated. Oh, beauty! comparable only to the moon—it is thus you have rendered me your slave.

III.

AIR—" RARTE."

Hitz bolounmaz boilé dilbaz
Néler etti bana bou yaz !
Ashikiné kaiet kournaz.

Nakarat.

Néler etti bana bou yaz

Pek kuchuk dur guirméz élé,
Bezmé guelir gulé gulé,
Guiounum pek outzdu hélé.

Bi vefadir inan olmaz,
Guioïnu olour bana sormaz,
Yani tez dir tekde dourmaz.

Bir hos éda inje sessi,
Alem bounun ufkendessi,
Guigmis basha oufak fessi.

It is impossible to find in the whole world so charming a prattler. What has she not done to me this summer! her disposition is to torment her lover.

Refrein.

What has she not done to me this summer!

She is too little to be taken in hand. She enters society laughing. On seeing her my heart flew towards her.

Useless girl! one cannot trust her—she does every thing she likes without consulting me—she is impatient, and never remains quiet.

She has an agreeable manner, and a sweet voice. All the world follows her steps. She wears on her head a fez.

IV.

AIR—" BEYATI ARÁBAN."

Niché bir askin-li feriat idéim?

Bir onoul masdahi derdim var benim

Soile messem derdim, aman né éiléim?

Sinemdé setr olounmas iaressi

Yokdour janim guiounumun mehparessi

Dem-bé-dem ah éilemekdir tzaressi

Hasretinli édérim feriatan—ah .

Vah ki oldou harmani Ennerum temessah

Benden vaz guel olman dadouah!

Hakdan dilerim yarzma ferman ola birgun

Ferman oloupda derdimé derman ola birgun.

Ister bou guonul yarile mejlis koura birgun

. Bir den tzéviré kebabi pir-yau ola birgun.

Vardim bagh-bana bir gul diledim vermedi bir gul
Gun olaki gul Eununedé narman ola bir gun.

Ei Ashik omer! tzektijéin askin éliden
Bir ben bilirim bir oulou sultan aga—yolloum
Nijé bir nijé sou elin kahri ?
Yeter oldou bou janima kiar etti
Kioutunun sozleri feléin kahri
Beni vetanimdan derbeder etti.

How long must I complain of my love? The
misery which consumes me is incurable. If I give not
vent to my sorrow, what shall I do? Brilliant object of my heart's love! you will not alleviate the
mortal wounds of my breast; my only resource, then,
is to groan and to sigh. Captivated by love for you,
I consume myself in useless complaints. How much
do I regret the life I am about to lose!

I hope my mistress will some day be condemned—
this would then assuage my pains.

I desire to find myself some day with my mistress, and to amuse myself with her at a fête in the country.

I went one day to a cultivator of vineyards, and asked him for a rose, which he refused me. I hope that roses will some day grow in my path.

Oh ! the many pains I suffer from love, no one but myself and my sultan are aware of. How long will they make me suffer these pains? I have borne enough—my soul is overcharged. The speeches of the wicked and the contrarieties of fortune have obliged me to quit my country, and to become a wanderer.

V.

AIR—" FANARAKI."

Aldi aklim bir sevekiar,
Guioununou seri ettin sikiar
Servi katdi nazik refdar.

Nakarat.

Pek jilveli bis sevekiar
Vasf olounmas boïlé bir i'ar.

Ebroulerim tire-keman,
Katzma benden ei nev jivan
Soïléissin derdé derman.

Sendé olan névazisler !
Iakti sinem o guelisler
Nim—niguiahin jané isler.

Sana ashik bi—bedeldir

—Rahat éilé ; ufkendé dir

Guiounu, guozu hep sendé dir.

TRANSLATION

A beauty ravished my soul—she has made a prey of my heart—her figure resembles the young cypress—her manners are all elegance.

Refrein.

Oh, beauty full of charms, it is impossible to describe such a friend

Your eyebrows resemble a bow. Oh, young beauty, fly not from me. Your words are a consolation to my sufferings.

Oh, how graceful you are! your approach has burnt my breast—Your half-looks have impressed themselves on the soul

Love cannot leave you —be tranquil—she is yours— her heart, her eyes, are fixed on you.

VI.

AIR—" RARTE."

Ewel benim gul héndanim

Kuchuk, amma, né janim.

Haïlé demdir guisrmeijeli

Né yapar, benim sultanim?

Nakarat.

Nassip Hanim, guel a janim!

Guel benim, yosma jivanim.

Oinariken guler bakar

Etrafina émir yapar

Dounia ona mejbour olsa

Guené éfendini arar.

TRANSLATION.

Oh, smiling rose! who from the commencement wast

mine. Little, but excessively charming! It is a long time since I have seen her. How is my sultana?

Refrein.

Oh, Lady Nassip, come, my beloved! come, girl full of attractions.

In dancing she looks about and laughs, and commands all who surround her. If even the whole world were at her feet she would still always seek out her lover.

Tevjihat, or list of the nomination of Pashas,
published in Zilkadi, 1249 *(March,* 1834.*)*

Ibrahim pasha confirmed in the government
of Abyssinia, in the Sanjak of Jeddah, and in
the functions of Sheikh el Harem of Mekkah.

Mehemmed Hosrew pasha confirmed in the
functions of Serasker of the regular troops,
and of governor-general of Constantinople.

Tahir pasha confirmed in the command of
the islands, and to the admiralty.

Ahmed pasha confirmed as commander-in-
chief of the troops of the Imperial Guard.

Halil Rifat pasha confirmed as director-general of artillery.

Husseyn pasha confirmed in the government-general of Rumelia, with the surveillance of the passes.

Mehemmed Ali pasha confirmed in the governments of Damascus, Egypt, Aleppo, Safed, Sayda, Beirout, and Tripoli of Syria.

Ali Riza pasha confirmed in the government of Baghdad, and of Bosra.

Mehemmed pasha confirmed in the government of Shehri-Zor.

Daood pasha confirmed in the government of Bosnia.

Esad pasha confirmed in the government of Arzeroom.

Resheed pasha, ex-grand-vizeer, confirmed to the government of Sivas, and the direction of the imperial mines.

Mirza Saed pasha, general of division of the line, confirmed to the government of Silistria,

and to the command of the fortress of Rous-
chuk.

Mehemmed Ali pasha confirmed to the government of the island of Crete, and to the
command of the fortress of Candia.

Othman pasha confirmed to the government
of Trebizond.

Elhaj Ali pasha confirmed to the government
of Karamania.

Ibrahim pasha, governor of Jeddah, confirmed to the government of Adana.

Iskak pasha confirmed to the government of
Diarbekir, and to that of Ricca.

Suleyman pasha, mirimiram, confirmed to the
government of Marash.

Ajarali Ahmed pasha, mirimiram, confirmed
to the government of Childir, to the government of Karz, and to the command of the fortress of that name.

Essad pasha, governor of Arzeroom, confirmed to the government of Vau, and to the command of the fortress of that name.

Saed pasha, mirimiram, confirmed to the government of Mosool.

Husseyn pasha, mirimiram, confirmed to the government of Tunis.

Yusuf pasha, mirimiram, confirmed to the government of Tripoli.

Mehemmed Ali pasha, governor of Egypt, confirmed to the sanjaks of Jerusalem and Nabloos.

Husseyn pasha confirmed to the sanjaks of Widin and Nicopolis, and to the command of the fortress of Widin.

Mustafa Noori pasha confirmed to the sanjak of Tricala.

Mahmood Hamdi pasha confirmed to the sanjaks of Yanina, Delvina, and Avlonia.

Hafiz pasha, general of division of the cavalry of the guard, confirmed to sanjak of
Scodra.

Vetzi pasha, confirmed to sanjak of Semen-
dria, and to the command of the fortress of
Belgrade.

Mehemmed Izzet pasha, ex-grand-vizeer, confirmed to sanjak of Kara Hissar Saheb.

Ahmed Khulusi pasha confirmed to sanjak
of Mentesheh.

Yakook pasha confirmed to sanjak of Aidin.

Mehemmed Raif pasha, general of division of infantry of the line, confirmed to sanjak
of Biga, and to the command of the straits
of the Dardanelles.

Eumer pasha confirmed to sanjak of Sa-
lonika.

Othman Noori pasha, mirimiram, confirmed
to sanjak of Caissar.

Resheed pasha, governor of Sivas, confirmed to sanjak of Choroom.

El haj Ali pasha, mirimiram, confirmed to sanjak of Tekkeh.

Saed Mehemmed Yeshar pasha, mirimiram, confirmed to sanjak of Uskiub.

Salih pasha confirmed to sanjaks of Keus-tendil and Doukakin, and to the command of the fortress of Nish.

Mahmood pasha, mirimiram, confirmed to sanjak of Prisren.

Daood pasha confirmed to sanjak of Kelis in Bosnia, and to sanjak of Soornik.

Ali pasha of Stolitza, confirmed to sanjak of Herseg.

Mehemmed Ali pasha, governor of Egypt, confirmed to sanjak of the Canea, and to the fortress of that name, also to the sanjak and fortress of Retimo.

Hajji Ali pasha, governor of Karamania, confirmed to sanjak of Ak Shehr.

Halil Rifat pasha, director-general of artillery, confirmed to sanjak of Alania.

Yusuf pasha, mirimiram, confirmed to sanjak of Ich Eli.

Besides the above, there are many sanjakleks farmed out, either by the general administration of the mookhataas, or by the administration of the mint, according to a list submitted to the approbation of the sultan.

The pasha of Egypt and his son, it will be observed, have between them the command of ten pashaleks, and six sanjakleks

LIST

OF THE

MINISTERS AND GRAND OFFICERS OF STATE

IN

THE TURKISH EMPIRE.

Vizeer Aadzem,   وزير اعظم
Prime Minister.

Mufty,   مفتي
Head of the Religion.

Kapoodan Pasha,   قپودان پاشا
Lord High Admiral.

Ser Aasker,   سرعسكر
Commander-in-Chief.

Reis Efendi,   ريس افندي
Minister for Foreign Affairs.

Kahia Bek,
Minister for the Home Department.

كحيا بك

Reis Al Ketab,
Secretary of State and Chancellor.

ريس الكتاب

Bash Defterdar,
Minister of Finances.

باش دفتردار

Chaoosh Bashi,
or Ahtesab Aghasi,
Minister of Police or Grand Marshal·

چاوش باشي
احتصاب اغاسي

Binyuk Telkheesji,
or Biuyuk Teskirezi,
Grand Maître des Requêtes. *

بيوك المخيصجي

Mektoobji Efendi,
Secretary to the Grand Vizeer.

مكتوبجي افندي

Ters-khaneh Emini,
Minister of the Navy.

ترسخانه اميني

---

* I have translated this into French, as I do not know what answers to it in English. The same is the case with respect to the office of Beklekji Efendi.

Dzereb-khaneh Emini,   ضربخانه اميني

Master of the Mint.

Defter-khaneh Emini,   دفترخانه اميني

Keeper of the Archives.

Nishanji Bashi,   نشانجي باشي

Keeper of the Seals.

Tesherifaji Bashi,   تشريفاجي باشي

Master of the Ceremonies.

Kahia Kiatibi,   كحيا كاتبي

Secretary of the Kahia.

Doulet Terjemani,   دولت ترجماني

Interpreter to the S. P.

Kapooji Bashi,   قپوجي باشي

Grand Chamberlain.

Kaeem-makam,   قايم مقام

Vice-Vizeer.)—He exercises his functions during the absence of the Grand Vizeer with
the army. This office is generally filled by
the Kahia Bek.

Beklekji Efendi,   بكلكجي افندي

Rapporteur d'Etat.

These officers are not placed in all cases in their proper order, as I do not know the exact degree of precedence attached to each.

GENEALOGICAL TABLE,

SHOWING

THE DESCENT OF THE PRESENT SULTAN MAHMOOD FROM ADAM.

1	Adam.	ادم صفي الله
2	Sheith.	شيث
3	Enosh.	انوش
4	Keenan.	قينان
5	Jehankeer.	جهانكير
6	Mehelathel.	مهلائل
7	Aberdeered.	ابرديرد

8	Adrees.	ادريس
9	Mooshtalekh.	موشخ
10	Malek Kerd.	ملك كرد
11	Noah.	نوح
12	Yafet.	يافت
13	Yelkhesan.	يلخسان
14	Macheen.	ماچين
15	Bedkhesan.	بدخسان
16	Sakerkoonjan.	سكرقونجان
17	Sakerthemoud.	سكرثمود
18	Batemour.	باتمور
19	Koorlugha.	قورلوغا
20	Karahool.	قره حول
21	Suleyman.	سليمان
22	Kara Oghlan.	قره اوغلان
23	Kemash.	قماش
24	Kerjah.	قرجه
25	Kertelmes.	قرتلمس

26 Harsoogha. حارسوغا

27 Meesertej. میسرتج

28 Tefral. طفرل

29 Hemarem. حمرم

30 Baeesoub. بایسوب

31 Soonj. سونج

32 Faly. فالي

33 Bash Bogha. باش بوغا

34 Yemak. یماق

35 Kooly. قولي

36 Koortelmesh. قورتلمش

37 Kazel Bogha. قزل بوغا

38 Kamery. قمري

39 Teraj. تراج

40 Bektum. بکتم

41 Kemar. قمار

42 Artak. ارتق

43 This name is obliterated in the MS.

44 Ai-dooghmesh.   اي دوغمش

45 Toorak.   توراق

46 Koutloo.   قوتلو

47 Karah.   قره

48 Arghoon.   ارغون

49 Aghoor.   اغوز

50 Kookeb.   كوكب

51 Yaeesouka.   يايسوقا

52 Bekeemoor.   بقيمور

53 Kiou Aaljan.   قيو علجان

54 Yafy Aasha.   يافي اعشا

55 Basneghoor.   باسنغور

56 Keersetem.   قيرستم

57 Bogha.   بوغا

58 Arghougha.   ارغوغا

59 Suljan.   سلجان

60 Koutloo.   قوتلو

61 ⎫
    ⎬ Two names obliterated in the MS.
62 ⎭

63	Karah.	قره
64	Artoghroul.	ارطغرول

SULTANS OF THE TURKISH EMPIRE.

65	Othman I.	عثمان
66	Aorkhan.	اورخان
67	Bayezeed I.	بايزيد
68	Muhammed I.	محمد
69	Murad II.	مراد
70	Muhammed II.	محمد
71	Bayezeed II.	بايزيد
72	Saleem I.	سليم
73	Suleyman I.	سليمان
74	Saleem II.	سليم
75	Murad III.	مراد
76	Muhammed III.	محمد
77	Ahmed I.	احمد

78 Murad IV.   مراد

79 Ibraheem I.   ابراهيم

80 Muhammed IV.   محمد

81 Ahmed II.   احمد

82 Abd al Hameed   عبدالحميد

83 Mahmood   محمود

In this list of names the reader will find many mentioned in the Bible, though somewhat changed; as, Sheith for Seth, Enosh for Enos, &c.

Receipt for making Coffee.

As coffee is as delicious a beverage in the Turkish dominions as it is detestable in all Frank countries, (which is proved by the inhabitants of the latter being obliged to mix it up with cream and sugar, in order to conceal its imperfections,) I have thought that a few words on the oriental mode of making it might be found useful. The proper selection of the bean forms, of course, the basis of the system ; and yet, perhaps, not so much so, as might at first be imagined ; for I have drunk excellent coffee made by Turks from inferior West India berries, and, on the other hand, have attempted in England to swallow an unpleasing decoction made from the very *élite* of Mokah beans. These ought to be small, of an even size and colour, and free from blemishes.

The selection being made, the berries are scattered on a large metal dish without a cover, and placed over a fourneau ; the coffee must be constantly moved about, as well as the dish itself, and the beans must not be in so great a number as to form in any part a double layer ; by not attending to this part of the process, they will repose too long in the same position, the dish will be unevenly heated in different parts, and some of the berries will not come in contact with the metal ; the natural consequence of this is, that in many instances they will be over, and in others under-roasted, and thereby destroy the flavour of the whole. One of the greatest faults with the Franks is over-roasting. If a fault cannot be avoided, let it proceed from the opposite cause. The reason why coffee should be placed in an open dish is self-evident, —the abominable iron cylinders, in which, throughout the rest of Europe, the berries are confined, become in a short time so heated interiorly that both the aroma and the essence of the coffee, in the form of a rich oil, is destroyed and dried up; this evil is avoided in the open dish, for the pressure of the atmospheric air represses the escape of these essential parts, and the bean is left moist and glossy with its own extract. I have seen cylinders in France formed with holes to allow some of the heat to escape; but this method, though apparently plausible in theory, is valueless in practice. No greater quantity of coffee should be roasted than is sufficient for each day's consumption.

You now proceed to reduce the berries into powder, and this is not done by means of a mill, but by pounding them in a mortar, for the simple reason that no mill can grind them sufficiently fine, and consequently the boiling water

is unable to extract their full flavour and sub-
stance. When well pounded it should be
passed through the finest sieve, and all that
does not go through should be again placed
in the mortar till the whole be reduced to an
impalpable powder.

The beverage itself is now made by placing
in a tin pot the required quantity of the powder
— and I would here observe, that each cup had
better be made separately; on the powder is
poured boiling water in the ratio of one-seventh
more than the quantity of the beverage wanted.
It must never be again permitted to boil, but
should be allowed to simmer; the pot is then
withdrawn, and having been tapped once or
twice against the hearth, is again replaced before
the fire : this is to be repeated five or six times.

Coffee, if properly made, should be covered
with foam or beads, when poured into the *fin-
jan*, or cup.

Instead of using plain water, a decoction of coffee is found preferable. In Turkish cafés the residue or deposit of every coffee-pot is thrown into a small cauldron containing hot water, and on a person asking for a cup of coffee the water is taken from this cauldron.

By strictly adhering to these few and simple rules, there can be no doubt that good coffee *ought* to be made. You should, of course, drink the beverage as hot as possible, and never, as Pope says,

"Over cold coffee trifle with the spoon.

THE END.

LONDON :
IBOTSON AND PALMER, PRINTERS, SAVOY STREET, STRAND.

CPSIA information can be obtained at www.ICGtesting.com
Printed in the USA
BVOW04s0355090215

386650BV00026B/163/P